VIA LATINA

Words

Peter Sipes

Student's name: _____

Pluteo Pleno · Chicago, Illinois

Via Latina: Words
Student workbook

Peter Sipes

Pluteo Pleno
5516 North Linder Avenue
Chicago, Illinois 60630

www.via-latina.com
www.pluteopleno.com

Cover image: Roadway at Itálica, Spain

This book would have been impossible without the support of Classical Consortium Academy of Barrington, Illinois. Especially Jennifer Burns, Angel Warner and Tammy Chapman. Thank you.

For my students. You inspire me.

Edition 1.0, July 2014

Coil bound: ISBN 978-1-937847-06-7
Paperback: ISBN 978-1-937847-07-4

Table of Contents

8th Milestone

Extras

Introduction

I've got a secret to tell you.

The language you speak, English, is a mutt of a langauge. It's got a Germanic grammar and a Latin vocabulary. As a result, there are all sorts of words you already know which come from Latin. Really easy words.

Doctor. Face.

They're all over English. In fact, words that trace their origins to Latin make up the majority of dictionary entries. In the previous sentence, these words came from Latin somehow: *fact, trace, origins, Latin, majority, dictionay, entries*. Pretty impressive, huh?

The next few pages are some business we need to take care of before we start with learning the words. Page vi is about how we learn about English words. I hope you find it interesting. Pages vii, viii, ix and x are about pronunciation of Latin. It's quite a bit of information. If you feel overwhelmed by that information, don't worry. I have videos pronouncing the words at

vialatinawords.blogspot.com

Latin is an exciting subject. I hope I can share a bit of that excitement with you.

Magister Petrus

Sicagi

Kal. Iul., AD 2014

How the Book Works

In this book you will be focusing on learning Latin words. It is not like learning English words. When you learn a new English word, you already know a thousands of English words to give your new word company. You also know English grammar really well. I'll teach you a new word as an example. I don't think you know one of the words in the next sentence:

Luckily, I knocked only one <u>bibelot</u> off of the shelf at Grandma's house.

So *bibelot*. Don't worry about what that means right now. Let's focus on what you know right away. First off you know it is a noun. If you can have one of something, it is a noun. It also means that you know what the plural is. Try it in this sentence.

Grandma has lots of _____.

Did you put in *bibelots*? I'm sure you did. So what else do we know? Well, since I said only one in the first sentence, a *bibelot* is probably something people have lots of. It might be small too—helpful if you're going to have a lot of them. It is also the sort of thing Grandma would own. So it probably isn't a baseball card or glow stick or school folder.

And that is my point. In English, new words have a grammatical home right away. Latin words won't at first, so you'll need to work hard.

But we still don't know what *bibelot* means. Ok, it means knick-knack. And you say it BE-below. The *t* is silent. So now you know what it means, you can make connections between the word *bibelot* and all the other words you know. You can remember (and this happens sort of without you trying to do it) that it goes with things like *Grandma, shelf,* and *knick-knack*. And you don't have that network of other words to go along with your new Latin words. So that will make it a little tricky too. But don't worry. You can do this. These new Latin words are probably also related to other English words.

Make sure you work at this every day. Learning a language is like learning math. You have to do a little bit every day. You have to practice. There are easy parts that you have to master before you can go on to the hard parts. But don't worry. Everyone has to start somewhere.

Pronunciation Guide

Two bits of good news: first, you already know the alphabet, and Latin is a phonetic language. So you pronounce it like it's written. Many, but not all, of the sounds that letters make are also going to be very familiar to you. Some will be quite different.

Consonants

All are like English consonants except:

c: always like the *c* in car
g: always like the *g* in gold
i: (when a consonant) like *y* in yet
m: see next page
q: always with *u*, like English
r: rolled like Spanish and Italian
s: always like *s* in snake
t: like *t* in top
v: like *w*
x: always like *x* in ax
z: like the *ds* like in fads

Consonant combinations

bs: like ps in tops
bt: like pt in apt
ch: like the ck-h in knock hard
gn: like *ni* in onion
ph: like the p-h in top hat
th: like the t-h in hot head

Double consonants

Pronounce each consonant. For example, the words *sumus* (we are) and *summus* (highest) sound different because one has one m and the other has two.

Vowels

a: like *o* in shot
ā: like *a* in father
e: like *e* in bet
ē: like *ay* in day
i: like *i* in in
ī: like *i* in machine
o: like the *aw* in raw
ō: like the *ow* in row
u: like *u* in dude
ū: like *oo* in food
y: say Latin *ī* while holding your lips like Latin *u* (yes, it's tricky)
ȳ: like Latin *y* but a bit longer

Diphthongs

   (Vowels in combination)
ae: like the English word I
au: like the English word ow
ei: like the *ay* in hay
eu: tricky, like hey you without the *h* and *y*
oe: like the *oi* in oil
ui: like the *ooey* in gooey

The letter M

Most of the time it is going to be just like the m in English. Whenever m is the first letter, it's just like the m in English. Whenever m is in the middle of a word, just like English.

But at the end of a word, it gets weird.

Something strange happens. The technical term is "nasalization." *You can ignore this effect if you want. You can pretend that it is like the m in English. It will be ok.* But if you nasalize final m, a few weird features of Latin will make sense now and when you go on to further study. Without futher ado, how to nasalize m.

Step 1: Make an n sound. Check where your tongue is. It should be on that ridge behind your teeth. The technical name for it is the alveolar ridge. Hold your finger under your nose. You should feel some air coming out.

Step 2: Make a Latin ē. Check where your tounge is. It should near the top and front of your mouth. Hold your finger under your nose. You shouldn't feel any air coming out.

Step 3: Do them both at the same time. Ok, a little trickier than that. Hold your tounge like the ē in step 2, then start making the n sound in step 1. You are now saying em, which is how you say um in Latin.

The only vowels that combine with m for this effect will be a (-am), e (-em) and u (-um). There's an i that makes -im, but it's pretty unusual. These combinations all count as long vowels, but that won't be important until you study poetry in Latin.

Trick of the trade: -om and -um sound similar enough that Latin says they are the same. (This will help you make some sense of what's going on in the second and fourth declensions' Accusative case when you get there.)

Macrons

To tell the truth, most of the time macrons—those marks over some vowels—won't make a bit of difference. I am going to use them anyway, because they do make a difference in how you say a word—well, we're not 100% sure what Latin sounded like, but we know for sure what difference the macron makes. Macrons will also help you figure out which word is which on occasion.

So just what difference do they make? A macron on a vowel makes it long. Long and short vowels in Latin are not like long and short vowels in English. In Latin it means that you hold onto the vowel for a bit longer if it is long. Your mouth may also feel a bit more open.

Sometimes it makes a difference in what the word does in a sentence:

aqua	aquā	fīlia	fīliā
water	water	daughter	daughter
SN	OP	SN	OP

(And the macron on the a in *aquā* and *fīliā* is one you may want to learn.)

Sometimes it completely changes a word's meaning:

hic	hīc	liber	līber
this	here	book	child
SN	adv		

Other times it can help sort out the differences in some bits of grammar:

mar*is*	equ*īs*	mur*e*	di*ē*
sea	horse	mouse	day
Genitive	Ablative	3rd declension	5th declension

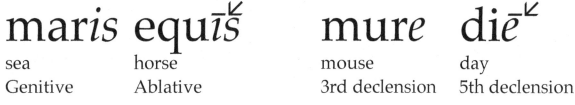

venit	vēnit
he comes	it came
Present tense	Perfect tense

Stress

Because you hear English every day, you know the ins and outs of its pronunciation. Particularly where stress goes in each word. With good reason: it can make a difference in what the word means. Like this:

pro*duce*
a verb: *make something*

produce
a noun: *fruits and veggies*

Now that you know how important that stress in pronouncing a word, let's learn the rules. They're simple.

1. One syllable word? Stress that syllable.
2. Two syllable word? Stress the first syllable.
3. Three or more syllable word? Stress falls on either the next to last syllable or the one before that. (Count back from the last syllable and those that are two and three are your suspects. No others.)
4. If the next to last syllable has a long vowel, diphthong or is closed, the stress sticks there.
5. Otherwise, on the syllable before that. But this, as usual, is easier to explain with examples.

First up: next to last syllable is long.

↙ *long*
vidēre
stress sticks on the long syllable
(means *to see*)

↙ *short*
*a*gere
stress moves back another syllable
(means *to do*)

Next up: next to last syllable is closed. First, what is a closed syllable? It is a syllable that ends with a consonant or consonant cluster. In the word *produce*, *pro-* is an open syllable and *-duce* is a closed syllable. Now for Latin examples.

↙ *open*
op*ti*mus
-ti- is an open syllable (no consonant)
stress moves back one syllable
(means *the best*)

↙ *closed*
agen*da*
-gen- is a closed syllable (consonant)
stress sticks here
(means *things to be done*)

Chapter 1
Nouns have case

Vōcēs

familia, familiae – 1f – family
fēmina, fēminae – 1f – woman
frāter, frātris – 3m – brother
māter, mātris – 3f – mother
parēns, parentis – 3m/f – parent
pater, patris – 3m – father
puella, puellae – 1f – girl
puer, puerī – 2m – boy
soror, sorōris – 3f – sister
vir, virī – 2m – man

Grammatica Latīna

Latin nouns have case. So what is case? Case is something that changes the spelling and pronunciation of a word depending on what it does in a sentence. English doesn't have case for most nouns, but it does with pronouns. Let's take a look.

> *He sees the dog.*
> *The dog sees him.*

Ok. All of the words are the same except for one. In the first sentence you have "he". In the second sentence you have "him". In the first sentence "he" is doing the seeing. In the second, the dog is doing the seeing. What does the dog see? "Him". The difference between *he* and *him* is case.

In your vocabulary words, you should see each word written twice. But they aren't quite the same, are they? The difference is case. Latin has five cases. You don't need to know their names or what they do right now, but you will learn them.

In your vocabulary words, you have the Nominative case and the Genitive case. This is the way that Latin students look words up in the dictionary. No matter what case the words is, you look for the Nominative case with the Genitive tagging along after. (And for now, don't worry about what they do past that.)

Pēnsa

Vōcēs memorandae
Fill in each blank with the definition supplied in *vōcēs*.

familia, familiae – 1f – _____

fēmina, fēminae – 1f – _____

frāter, frātris – 3m – _____

māter, mātris – 3f – _____

parēns, parentis – 3m/f – _____

pater, patris – 3m – _____

puella, puellae – 1f – _____

puer, puerī – 2m – _____

soror, sororis – 3f – _____

vir, virī – 2m – _____

Using the vōcēs
Circle the right answer.

1. Which one are you? Puella Puer

2. Which one is your *māter*? Fēmina Vir

3. Which one is your *pater*? Fēmina Vir

4. If you are *soror*, which are you? Puella Puer

5. If you are *frāter*, which are you? Puella Puer

6. Who is *parēns*? Puer Vir

7. Who is *parēns*? Puella Fēmina

8. Draw a picture of your family and write two of the *vōcēs* about every person in your family.

Derivative practice

Look for the Latin word in the *vōcēs* that goes with the English derivative. Then look the derivative up in your dictionary.

Latin word	English derivative	What the derivative means
	family	
	parent	
	fraternity	
	sorority	

3

Probātiō

Vōcēs memorātae
Fill in the definition for each word.

familia, familiae – 1f – _____

fēmina, fēminae – 1f – _____

frāter, frātris – 3m – _____

māter, mātris – 3f – _____

parēns, parentis – 3m / f – _____

pater, patris – 3m – _____

puella, puellae – 1f – _____

puer, puerī – 2m – _____

soror, sorōris – 3f – _____

vir, virī – 2m – _____

Chapter 2
Nouns have number and gender

Vōcēs

discipula, discipulae – 1f – student (girl)
discipulus, discipulī – 2m – student (boy)
fābula, fābulae – 1f – story
historia, historiae – 1f – history
liber, librī – 2m – book
magister, magistrī – 2m – teacher (man)
magistra, magistrae – 1f – teacher (woman)
penna, pennae – 1f – pen
schola, scholae – 1f – school
sella, sellae – 1f – chair

Grammatica Latīna

Nouns have number. Number is just like English—singular (one) or plural (more than one). Latin has a different system for showing number than English does, but the idea is the same. Singular—one. Plural—more than one.

Gender is another story. In our vocabulary list you can see the difference between boy and girl students and man and woman teachers. That's easy enough. And you can see the gender difference in two places.

discupula, discipulae – 1f – student (girl)
discipulus, discipulī – 2m – student (boy)

But wait! What's this?

penna, pennae – 1f – pen

Pens are feminine? Yes. In Latin they are. Every noun has gender, and you can't predict it. You will have to memorize it with each new word. Lucky for you, the letter between the Latin word and the English definition tells you the word's gender. There are three. M is for masculine. F is for feminine. N is for Neuter

Pēnsa

Vōcēs memorandae
Fill in each blank with the definition supplied in *vōcēs*.

discipula, discipulae – 1f – _____

discipulus, discipulī – 2m – _____

fābula, fābulae – 1f – _____

historia, historiae – 1f – _____

liber, librī – 2m – _____

magister, magistrī – 2m – _____

magistra, magistrae – 1f – _____

penna, pennae – 1f – _____

schola, scholae – 1f – _____

sella, sellae – 1f – _____

Using the vōcēs
Circle the right answer.

1. Which one of these do you use to write? Penna Liber

2. Which one of these do you read? Penna Liber

3. Who teaches? Magister Discipulus

4. Who learns? Magistra Discipula

5. What subject is about the past? Fābula Historia

6. Where do you sit? Discipulus Sella

7. What might be in a liber? Fabula Penna

8. Draw a picture of your school and label it with at least seven different *vōcēs*.

Derivative practice

Look for the Latin word in the *vōcēs* that goes with the English derivative. Then look the derivative up in your dictionary.

Latin word	English derivative	What the derivative means
	disciple	
	fable	
	pen	
	school	

Probātiō

Vōcēs memorātae
Fill in the definition for each word.

discipula, discipulae – 1f – _____

discipulus, discipulī – 2m – _____

fābula, fābulae – 1f – _____

historia, historiae – 1f – _____

liber, librī – 2m – _____

magister, magistrī – 2m – _____

magistra, magistrae – 1f – _____

penna, pennae – 1f – _____

schola, scholae – 1f – _____

sella, sellae – 1f – _____

Chapter 3
Nouns have declension

Vōcēs

ager, agrī – 2m – field
aqua, aquae – 1f – water
arbor, arboris – 3f – tree
flōs, flōris – 3m – flower
fluvius, fluviī – 2m – river
īnsula, īnsulae – 1f – island
oceanus, oceanī – 2m – ocean
sōl, sōlis – 3m – sun
urbs, urbis – 3If* – city
via, viae – 1f – road

Grammatica Latīna

Ok. So what's that little number next to the gender? That's the declension number. Latin has five declension of nouns. Wait. Declension? Yeah, it's a group of nouns that share all have the same endings. We don't have much of it in English, but here's an idea of how it works.

ENGLISH DECLENSION	S	Z	EN
Singular	book	dog	child
Possessive	book's	dog'z	child's
Plural	books	dogz	children
Possessive	books'	dogz'	children's

Of course we don't spell *dogs* as *dogz*, but we do say it that way. So what other words go in the *s* declension? *Rat. Track. Lap.* What else goes in the *z* declension? *Car. Wheel. Tree.* What else goes in the *en* declension? Almost nothing. *Ox. Brother* used to when it was *bretheren*, but now it's shifted over to the *z* declension as *brothers*.

If that's confusing, think of it like a family that a noun belongs to. They don't look completely alike, but in some ways they do. In Latin, they rhyme.

*3If – third declension i-stem feminine. I-stem is a group within a group.

Pēnsa

Vōcēs memorandae
Fill in each blank with the definition supplied in *vōcēs*.

ager, agrī – 2m – _____

aqua, aquae – 1f – _____

arbor, arboris – 3f – _____

flōs, flōris – 3m – _____

fluvius, fluviī – 2m – _____

īnsula, īnsulae – 1f – _____

oceanus, oceanī – 2m – _____

sōl, sōlis – 3m – _____

urbs, urbis – 3If – _____

via, viae – 1f – _____

Using the vōcēs
Circle the right answer.

1. Which one smells nice? Flos Urbs

2. Which one of these could you swim across? Fluvius Oceanus

3. Which one can protect you from *sōl*? Arbor Īnsula

4. Which one is in *urbs*? Oceanus Via

5. Which one is in the sky? Īnsula Sōl

6. Which one can you drink? Aqua Ager

7. Where might you see horses? Ager Oceanus

8. Draw a picture of the outdoors and label it with at least eight different *vōcēs*.

Derivative practice

Look for the Latin word in the *vōcēs* that goes with the English derivative. Then look the derivative up in your dictionary.

Latin word	English derivative	What the derivative means
	acre	
	floral	
	ocean	
	solar	

Probātiō

Vōcēs memorātae
Fill in the definition for each word.

ager, agrī – 2m – _____

aqua, aquae – 1f – _____

arbor, arboris – 3f – _____

flōs, flōris – 3m – _____

fluvius, fluviī – 2m – _____

īnsula, īnsulae – 1f – _____

oceanus, oceanī – 2m – _____

sōl, sōlis – 3m – _____

urbs, urbis – 3If – _____

via, viae – 1f – _____

Vōcēs

ager, agrī – 2m – field

aqua, aquae – 1f – water

arbor, arboris – 3f – tree

discipula, discipulae – 1f – student (girl)

discipulus, discipulī – 2m – student (boy)

fābula, fābulae – 1f – story

familia, familiae – 1f – family

fēmina, fēminae – 1f – woman

frāter, frātris – 3m – brother

flōs, flōris – 3m – flower

fluvius, fluviī – 2m – river

historia, historiae – 1f – history

īnsula, īnsulae – 1f – island

liber, librī – 2m – book

magister, magistrī – 2m – teacher (man)

magistra, magistrae – 1f – teacher (woman)

māter, mātris – 3f – mother

oceanus, oceanī – 2m – ocean

parēns, parentis – 3m / f – parent

pater, patris – 3m – father

penna, pennae – 1f – pen

puella, puellae – 1f – girl

puer, puerī – 2m – boy

sōl, sōlis – 3m – sun

schola, scholae – 1f – school

sella, sellae – 1f – chair

soror, sororis – 3f – sister

via, viae – 1f – road

vir, virī – 2m – man

urbs, urbis – 3If – city

Grammatica Latīna

So we know that each Latin noun has four things.

Case — That's the difference between *she* and *her*. It changed with how the word is used in a sentence.

Number — That's the difference between *dog* and *dogs*.

Gender — English nouns don't really have this, but every Latin noun does.

Declension — It's like a family for nouns.

The first two—Case and Number—are special for grammar reasons. They can change. The second two—Gender and Declension—cannot change. They are always the same.

Here is a sample glossary entry showing you where all of these pieces are.

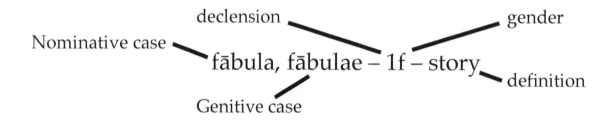

Now and then you might see something that is odd. A word might have two very different definitions or a declension you don't know. That's not a problem. Just learn the words and trust that the strange information is right.

In the next few chapters, we'll look at the declensions.

Pēnsa

Vōcēs memorandae
Fill in each blank with the definition supplied in *vōcēs*.

ager, agrī – 2m – _____   magistra, magistrae – 1f – _____

aqua, aquae – 1f – _____   māter, mātris – 3f – _____

arbor, arboris – 3f – _____   oceanus, oceanī – 2m – _____

discipula, discipulae – 1f – _____   parēns, parentis – 3m/f – _____

discipulus, discipulī – 2m – _____   pater, patris – 3m – _____

fābula, fābulae – 1f – _____   penna, pennae – 1f – _____

familia, familiae – 1f – _____   puella, puellae – 1f – _____

fēmina, fēminae – 1f – _____   puer, puerī – 2m – _____

flōs, flōris – 3m – _____   schola, scholae – 1f – _____

fluvius, fluviī – 2m – _____   sella, sellae – 1f – _____

frāter, frātris – 3m – _____   sōl, sōlis – 3m – _____

historia, historiae – 1f – _____   soror, sorōris – 3f – _____

īnsula, īnsulae – 1f – _____   urbs, urbis – 3If – _____

liber, librī – 2m – _____   via, viae – 1f – _____

magister, magistrī – 2m – _____   vir, virī – 2m – _____

Derivative practice

Look for the Latin word in the *vōcēs* that goes with the English derivative. Then look the derivative up in your dictionary.

Latin word	English derivative	What the derivative means
	library	
	paternal	
	maternal	
	virile	

What makes these go together?

Each group of Latin words has another Latin word in common. What is that word?

_____ 1. Īnsula, Oceanus, Fluvius   a. Familia

_____ 2. Discipulus, Frater   b. Schola

_____ 3. Liber, Sella, Penna   c. Fēmina

_____ 4. Māter, Magistra   d. Aqua

_____ 5. Pater, Frater, Soror   e. Parēns

_____ 6. Pater, Māter   f. Puer

Chapter 5
There are more than nouns

Vōcēs

aestās, aestātis – 3f – summer
annus, annī – 2m – year
diēs, diēī – 5m – day
hodiē – adv – today
māne – 3n – morning
meridiēs, meridiēī – 5m – noon
nox, noctis – 3f – night
prīmus, prīma, prīmum – adj – first
tempus, temporis – 3n – time
ultimus, ultima, ultimum – adj – last

Grammatica Latīna

I doubt it is any surprise, but Latin doesn't just have nouns. It also has adjectives (adj) and adverbs (adv). You can see that their glossary entries are a little bit different from the nouns. Adverbs only have one word to memorize! Adjectives have three—but where did gender go? Hmmmm. Each one of the words you memorize for adjectives represents one of the genders. Why? Because Latin adjectives match their nouns in case, number and gender. Don't worry about this now, but you'll need to know that later.

Latin also has verbs (V, Vt, LV), conjunctions (C), prepositions (P) and pronouns. They aren't in this chapter, so don't worry about them just yet. We will be seeing them soon enough.

Pēnsa

Vōcēs memorandae
Fill in each blank with the definition supplied in *vōcēs*.

aestās, aestātis – 3f – _____

annus, annī – 2m – _____

diēs, diēī – 5m – _____

hodiē – adv – _____

māne – 3n – _____

meridiēs, meridiēī – 5m – _____

nox, noctis – 3f – _____

prīmus, prīma, prīmum – adj – _____

tempus, temporis – 3n – _____

ultimus, ultima, ultimum – adj – _____

Using the vōcēs
Circle the right answer.

1. Which one is shorter? Aestās Annus

2. Which one is longer? Diēs Annus

3. When do you wake up? Māne Meridiēs

4. When do you sleep? Meridiēs Nox

5. Which would you rather be in a race? Prīmus Ultimus

6. When are you doing your work? Hodiē Tempus

7. When are bats and owls asleep? Diēs Nox

8. Draw a picture that shows at least six different *vōcēs*. Label it.

Derivative practice

Look for the Latin word in the *vōcēs* that goes with the English derivative. Then look the derivative up in your dictionary.

Latin word	English derivative	What the derivative means
	annual	
	meridian	
	nocturnal	
	ultimate	

Probātiō

Vōcēs memorātae
Fill in the definition for each word.

aestās, aestātis – 3f – _____

annus, annī – 2m – _____

diēs, diēī – 5m – _____

hodiē – adv – _____

māne – 3n – _____

meridiēs, meridiēī – 5m – _____

nox, noctis – 3f – _____

prīmus, prīma, prīmum – adj – _____

tempus, temporis – 3n – _____

ultimus, ultima, ultimum – adj – _____

Chapter 6
The cases

Vōcēs

auctor, auctōris – 3m – author
captīvus, captīvī – 2m – prisoner
dux, ducis – 3m – leader
mīles, mīlitis – 3m – soldier
nauta, nautae – 1m – sailor
poeta, poetae – 1m – poet
rēgīna, rēgīnae – 1f – queen
rēx, rēgis – 3m – king
scriptor, scriptōris – 3m – writer
uxor, uxōris – 3f – wife

Grammatica Latīna

It is time for you to learn the names of the cases. Don't worry about what they do. You'll cover that later (and a tiny bit in this book). For now, you should know their names. There are five cases. You already know two.

Nominative
Genitive

Those are the cases that are in the vocabulary entries. The other three are:

Dative
Accusative
Ablative

Since they're just names, it might help you to have a sentence to help your memory. Here's one:

Never Give Davus Any Apples

It lines up this way.

Never	Give	Davus	Any	Apples
Nominative	Genitive	Dative	Accusative	Ablative

Pēnsa

Vōcēs memorandae
Fill in each blank with the definition supplied in *vōcēs*.

auctor, auctōris – 3m – _____

captīvus, captīvī – 2m – _____

dux, ducis – 3m – _____

mīles, mīlitis – 3m – _____

nauta, nautae – 1m – _____

poeta, poetae – 1m – _____

rēgīna, rēgīnae – 1f – _____

rēx, rēgis – 3m – _____

scriptor, scriptōris – 3m – _____

uxor, uxōris – 3f – _____

Using the vōcēs
Circle the right answer.

1. Which *scriptor* writes poetry? Auctor Poeta

2. Who could be *uxor* too? Rēgīna Rēx

3. Who is in jail? Captīvus Nauta

4. Who is in the army? Mīles Nauta

5. Who is in charge? Captīvus Dux

6. Who wears a crown? Nauta Rēx

7. Who would you find on a boat? Nauta Scriptor

8. Fill out the chart with the cases.

Never	Give	Davus	Any	Apples

9. Draw a picture of a crowd of people. Everyone should have at least one label from the *vōces*.

[blank box for drawing]

Derivative practice

Look for the Latin word in the *vōcēs* that goes with the English derivative. Then look the derivative up in your dictionary.

Latin word	English derivative	What the derivative means
	military	
	nautical	
	regal	
	script	

Probātiō

Vōcēs memorātae

Fill in the definition for each word.

auctor, auctōris – 3m – _____

captīvus, captīvī – 2m – _____

dux, ducis – 3m – _____

mīles, mīlitis – 3m – _____

nauta, nautae – 1m – _____

poeta, poetae – 1m – _____

rēgīna, rēgīnae – 1f – _____

rēx, rēgis – 3m – _____

scriptor, scriptōris – 3m – _____

uxor, uxōris – 3f – _____

Fill out the chart with the cases.

Never	Give	Davus	Any	Apples

Chapter 7
1st Declension

Vōcēs

casa, casae – 1f –house
cēna, cēnae – 1f – supper
cibus, cibī – 2m – food
cista, cistae – 1f – box
cubiculum, cubiculī – 2n – bedroom
culīna, culīnae – 1f – kitchen
fructus, fructūs – 4m – fruit
lectus, lectī – 2m – bed
mēnsa, mēnsae – 1f – table
porta, portae – 1f – gate

Grammatica Latīna

Now for our first foray into learning some Latin endings. We're going to start with the first declension. A lot of the words on this list are first declension too. Look at them for a second. You should see three things.

1. They all end in -a.
2. The second word (Genitive case) ends in -ae.
3. They are all feminine. (There are few exceptions. See the vocab on p. 21.)

These are the endings for the first declension.

	Singular					Plural				
	Nom.	Gen.	Dat.	Acc.	Abl.	Nom.	Gen.	Dat.	Acc.	Abl.
1st	-a	-ae	-ae	-am	-ā	-ae	-ārum	-īs	-ās	-īs

But you never run across the endings on their own. They are always attached to a root. Here's an example.

	Nom.	Gen.	Dat.	Acc.	Abl.
Singular	casa	casae	casae	casam	casā
Plural	casae	casārum	casīs	casās	casīs

Pēnsa

Vōcēs memorandae

Fill in each blank with the definition supplied in *vōcēs*.

casa, casae – 1f – _____

cēna, cēnae – 1f – _____

cibus, cibī – 2m – _____

cista, cistae – 1f – _____

cubiculum, cubiculī – 2n – _____

culīna, culīnae – 1f – _____

fructus, fructūs – 4m – _____

lectus, lectī – 2m – _____

mēnsa, mēnsae – 1f – _____

porta, portae – 1f – _____

Using the vōcēs

Circle the right answer.

1. Which one is in a culīna? Casa Mēnsa

2. Which one might be on a *mēnsa*? Cibus Cubiculum

3. Which one is *cibus*? Fructus Lectus

4. Where would you rather sleep? Lectus Porta

5. How might you go outside? Cēna Porta

6. Where do you store things? Cibus Cista

7. Where is a lectus likely to be? Cubiculum Porta

8. Complete the chart for the 1st declension.

	Singular					Plural				
	Nom.	*Gen.*	*Dat.*	*Acc.*	*Abl.*	*Nom.*	*Gen.*	*Dat.*	*Acc.*	*Abl.*
1st										

9. Draw a picture of a house or kitchen and label it with at least eight *vōcēs*.

Derivative practice

Look for the Latin word in the *vōcēs* that goes with the English derivative. Then look the derivative up in your dictionary.

Latin word	English derivative	What the derivative means
	culinary	
	fruit	
	mesa	
	portal	

Probātiō

Vōcēs memorātae
Fill in the definition for each word.

casa, casae – 1f – _____

cēna, cēnae – 1f – _____

cibus, cibī – 2m – _____

cista, cistae – 1f – _____

cubiculum, cubiculī – 2n – _____

culīna, culīnae – 1f – _____

fructus, fructūs – 4m – _____

lectus, lectī – 2m – _____

mēnsa, mēnsae – 1f – _____

porta, portae – 1f – _____

Complete the chart for the 1st declension.

	Singular					Plural				
	Nom.	Gen.	Dat.	Acc.	Abl.	Nom.	Gen.	Dat.	Acc.	Abl.
1st										

Vōcēs

aestās, aestātis – 3f – summer

annus, annī – 2m – year

auctor, auctōris – 3m – author

captīvus, captīvī – 2m – prisoner

casa, casae – 1f –house

cēna, cēnae – 1f – supper

cibus, cibī – 2m – food

cista, cistae – 1f – box

cubiculum, cubiculī – 2n – bedroom

culīna, culīnae – 1f – kitchen

diēs, diēī – 5m – day

dux, ducis – 3m – leader

fructus, fructūs – 4m – fruit

lectus, lectī – 2m – bed

mēnsa, mēnsae – 1f – table

porta, portae – 1f – gate

hodiē – adv – today

māne – 3n – morning

meridiēs, meridiēī – 5m – noon

mīles, mīlitis – 3m – soldier

nauta, nautae – 1m – sailor

nox, noctis – 3f – night

poeta, poetae – 1m –poet

prīmus, prīma, prīmum – adj – first

rēgīna, rēgīnae – 1f – queen

rēx, rēgis – 3m – king

scriptor, scriptōris – 3m – writer

tempus, temporis – 3n – time

ultimus, ultima, ultimum – adj – last

uxor, uxōris – 3f – wife

Grammatica Latīna

In this unit we learned that Latin has more than just nouns. It has all the sorts of words you would expect a language to have. Adjectives, Verbs, Adverbs, Pronouns. All that stuff. Even so, we are going to focus mostly on nouns.

We also learned that there are five cases, just like there are five declensions. You can remember the names of the cases with this sentence.

Never Give Davus Any Apples

The names of the cases begin with the same letter as each of the words in the helper sentence.

Never	Give	Davus	Any	Apples
Nominative	Genitive	Dative	Accusative	Ablative

We also learned the endings that go with those cases for the first declension.

	Singular					Plural				
	Nom.	*Gen.*	*Dat.*	*Acc.*	*Abl.*	*Nom.*	*Gen.*	*Dat.*	*Acc.*	*Abl.*
1st	-a	-ae	-ae	-am	-ā	-ae	-ārum	-īs	-ās	-īs

Of course the endings never show upon their own. After all, the endings aren't words, so they've got to attach to something. Kind of like this.

	Nom.	*Gen.*	*Dat.*	*Acc.*	*Abl.*
Singular	casa	casae	casae	casam	casā
Plural	casae	casārum	casīs	casās	casīs

Pēnsa

Vōcēs memorandae

Fill in each blank with the definition supplied in *vōcēs*.

aestās, aestātis – 3f – _____

annus, annī – 2m – _____

auctor, auctōris – 3m – _____

captīvus, captīvī – 2m – _____

casa, casae – 1f – _____

cēna, cēnae – 1f – _____

cibus, cibī – 2m – _____

cista, cistae – 1f – _____

cubiculum, cubiculī – 2n – _____

_____

culīna, culīnae – 1f – _____

diēs, diēī – 5m – _____

dux, ducis – 3m – _____

fructus, fructūs – 4m – _____

lectus, lectī – 2m – _____

mēnsa, mēnsae – 1f – _____

porta, portae – 1f – _____

hodiē – adv – _____

māne – 3n – _____

meridiēs, meridiēī – 5m – _____

mīles, mīlitis – 3m – _____

nauta, nautae – 1m – _____

nox, noctis – 3f – _____

poeta, poetae – 1m – _____

prīmus, prīma, prīmum – adj – _____

_____

rēgīna, rēgīnae – 1f – _____

rēx, rēgis – 3m – _____

scriptor, scriptōris – 3m – _____

_____

tempus, temporis – 3n – _____

ultimus, ultima, ultimum – adj – _____

_____

uxor, uxōris – 3f – _____

Derivative practice

Look for the Latin word in the *vōcēs* that goes with the English derivative. Then look the derivative up in your dictionary.

Latin word	English derivative	What the derivative means
	A.M.	
	cubicle	
	duke	
	prime	

What makes these go together?

Each group of Latin words has another Latin word in common. What is that word?

_____ 1. Lectus, Mēnsa, Sella   a. Vir

_____ 2. Cibus, Fructus, Mēnsa   b. Culīna

_____ 3. Diēs, Māne, Nox   c. Cubiculum

_____ 4. Dux, Rēx, Nauta   d. Tempus

_____ 5. Rēgīna, Uxor   e. Fēmina

_____ 6. Lectus, Nox   f. Casa

Fill out the chart with the cases.

Never	Give	Davus	Any	Apples

Chapter 9
2nd Declension M

Vōcēs

caelum, caelī – 2n – sky

ecclēsia, ecclēsiae – 1f – church

equus, equī – 2m – horse

fōns, fontis – 3m – fountain

fundus, fundī – 2m – farm

negōtium, negōtiī – 2n – business

oppidum, oppidī – 2n – town

portus, portūs – 4m – port

rūs, rūris – 3n – country(side)

templum, templī – 2n – temple

Grammatica Latīna

Ok. Back to learning new things. This time we learn the 2nd declension masculine. There's no 2nd declension feminine, but there is a 2nd declension neuter. It will be in the next chapter.

	Singular					Plural				
	Nom.	*Gen.*	*Dat.*	*Acc.*	*Abl.*	*Nom.*	*Gen.*	*Dat.*	*Acc.*	*Abl.*
2nd M	-us	-ī	-ō	-um	-ō	-ī	-ōrum	-īs	-ōs	-īs

Once again, the endings never show upon their own. This is how the word *fundus* declines—that's how we say goes into all of its cases.

	Nom.	*Gen.*	*Dat.*	*Acc.*	*Abl.*
Singular	fundus	fundī	fundō	fundum	fundō
Plural	fundī	fundōrum	fundīs	fundōs	fundīs

Pēnsa

Vōcēs memorandae
Fill in each blank with the definition supplied in *vōcēs*.

caelum, caelī – 2n – _____

ecclēsia, ecclēsiae – 1f – _____

equus, equī – 2m – _____

fōns, fontis – 3m – _____

fundus, fundī – 2m – _____

negōtium, negōtiī – 2n – _____

oppidum, oppidī – 2n – _____

portus, portūs – 4m – _____

rūs, rūris – 3n – _____

templum, templī – 2n – _____

Using the vōcēs
Circle the right answer.

1. Which is likely to be on a *fundus*? Equus Portus

2. Where is *ecclēsia* more likely to be? Fōns Oppidum

3. Where are the stars? Caelum Fundus

4. What needs to be by *aqua*? Portus Templum

5. Where is *negōtium* likely to happen? Fōns Oppidum

6. Where might you find cows? Oppidum Rūs

7. Which is bigger? Caelum Templum

8. Complete the chart for the 2nd declension M.

	Singular					Plural				
	Nom.	*Gen.*	*Dat.*	*Acc.*	*Abl.*	*Nom.*	*Gen.*	*Dat.*	*Acc.*	*Abl.*
2nd M										

9. Draw a picture of the outdoors label it with at least eight *vōcēs*.

Derivative practice

Look for the Latin word in the *vōcēs* that goes with the English derivative. Then look the derivative up in your dictionary.

Latin word	English derivative	What the derivative means
	fountain	
	port	
	rural	
	temple	

Probātiō

Vōcēs memorātae
Fill in the definition for each word.

caelum, caelī – 2n – _____

ecclēsia, ecclēsiae – 1f – _____

equus, equī – 2m – _____

fōns, fontis – 3m – _____

fundus, fundī – 2m – _____

negōtium, negōtiī – 2n – _____

oppidum, oppidī – 2n – _____

portus, portūs – 4m – _____

rūs, rūris – 3n – _____

templum, templī – 2n – _____

Complete the chart for the 2nd declension masculine.

	Singular					Plural				
	Nom.	Gen.	Dat.	Acc.	Abl.	Nom.	Gen.	Dat.	Acc.	Abl.
2nd M										

Chapter 10
2nd Declension N

Vōcēs

ars, artis – 3f – skill
auxilium, auxiliī – 2n – help
causa, causae – 1f – cause
cōnsilium, cōnsiliī – 2n – plan
dōnum, dōnī – 2n – gift
epistula, epistulae – 1f – letter
nihil – n – nothing
perīculum, perīculī – 2n – danger
respōnsum, respōnsī – 2n – answer
verbum, verbī – 2n – word

Grammatica Latīna

This time up we learn the 2nd declension neuter. The cool thing about this group is that the Nominative and Accusative are the same.

	Singular					Plural				
	Nom.	Gen.	Dat.	Acc.	Abl.	Nom.	Gen.	Dat.	Acc.	Abl.
2nd N	-um	-ī	-ō	-um	-ō	-a	-ōrum	-īs	-a	-īs

As usual, the endings never show upon their own. With no further ado, 2nd declension neuter.

	Nom.	Gen.	Dat.	Acc.	Abl.
Singular	verbum	verbī	verbō	verbum	verbō
Plural	verba	verbōrum	verbīs	verba	verbīs

Pēnsa

Vōcēs memorandae
Fill in each blank with the definition supplied in *vōcēs*.

ars, artis – 3f – _____

auxilium, auxiliī – 2n – _____

causa, causae – 1f – _____

cōnsilium, cōnsiliī – 2n – _____

dōnum, dōnī – 2n – _____

epistula, epistulae – 1f – _____

nihil – n – _____

perīculum, perīculī – 2n – _____

respōnsum, respōnsī – 2n –_____

verbum, verbī – 2n – _____

Using the vōcēs
Circle the right answer.

1. Which would be a better *dōnum*? Auxilium Perīculum

2. Which would you learn? Ars Nihil

3. If you get *epistula*, what might you send back? Causa Respōnsum

4. Which one does *perīculum* have? Causa Verbum

5. What is this page covered in? Dōnum Verbum

6. Which one do you make before you do? Cōnsilium Nihil

7. What might you open on your birthday? Ars Dōnum

8. Complete the chart for the 2nd declension N.

	Singular					Plural				
	Nom.	Gen.	Dat.	Acc.	Abl.	Nom.	Gen.	Dat.	Acc.	Abl.
2nd N										

9. Draw a picture of a desk and label it with at least six *vōcēs*. (Some of these are tricky to draw.)

Derivative practice

Look for the Latin word in the *vōcēs* that goes with the English derivative. Then look the derivative up in your dictionary.

Latin word	English derivative	What the derivative means
	art	
	donation	
	nil	
	peril	

Probātiō

Vōcēs memorātae
Fill in the definition for each word.

ars, artis – 3f – _____

auxilium, auxiliī – 2n – _____

causa, causae – 1f – _____

cōnsilium, cōnsiliī – 2n – _____

donum, donī – 2n – _____

epistula, epistulae – 1f – _____

nihil – n – _____

perīculum, perīculī – 2n – _____

respōnsum, respōnsī – 2n –_____

verbum, verbī – 2n – _____

Complete the chart for the 2nd declension neuter.

	Singular					Plural				
	Nom.	Gen.	Dat.	Acc.	Abl.	Nom.	Gen.	Dat.	Acc.	Abl.
2nd N										

Chapter 11
3rd Declension M & F

Vōcēs

corpus, corporis – 3n – body
digitus, digitī – 2m – finger
faciēs, faciēī – 5f – face
lingua, linguae – 1f – tongue
manus, manūs – 4f – hand
memoria, memoriae – 1f – memory
oculus, oculī – 2m – eye
pēs, pedis – 3m – foot
vox, vōcis – 3f – voice
vultus, vultūs – 4m – face

Grammatica Latīna

Now up is the 3rd declension, masculine and feminine. In the 1st and 2nd M declensions, they had different endings. In the 3rd M/F declension, they've got the same endings. I suppose you see what is going to make this tricky. In the 2nd M declension, you don't need to really know the gender. Here you do.

	Singular					Plural				
	Nom.	Gen.	Dat.	Acc.	Abl.	Nom.	Gen.	Dat.	Acc.	Abl.
3rd M/F	*	-is	-ī	-em	-e	-ēs	-um	-ibus	-ēs	-ibus
	* Third declension has lots of possible endings, but ending with an "s" is very common.									

And then there's the Nominative singular. It's a * and not a proper ending, so you really do have to learn both forms in the vōcēs list. And the gender too!

	Nom.	Gen.	Dat.	Acc.	Abl.
Singular	vox	vōcis	vōcī	vōcem	vōce
Plural	vōcēs	vōcum	vōcibus	vōcēs	vōcibus

Pēnsa

Vōcēs memorandae
Fill in each blank with the definition supplied in *vōcēs*.

corpus, corporis – 3n – _____

digitus, digitī – 2m – _____

faciēs, faciēī – 5f – _____

lingua, linguae – 1f – _____

manus, manūs – 4f – _____

memoria, memoriae – 1f – _____

oculus, oculī – 2m – _____

pēs, pedis – 3m – _____

vox, vōcis – 3f – _____

vultus, vultūs – 4m – _____

Using the vōcēs
Circle the right answer.

1. Where is *digitus*? Manus Vox

2. Where is *oculus*? Digitus Vultus

3. What do *manus* and *vultus* have in common? Corpus Memoria

4. What do you have two of? Lingua Manus

5. Which would you use to talk about yesterday? Memoria Meus

6. Which one is in *faciēs*? Lingua Pes

7. Which do you have more of? Digitus Oculus

8. Complete the chart for the 3rd declension M/F.

	Singular					Plural				
	Nom.	*Gen.*	*Dat.*	*Acc.*	*Abl.*	*Nom.*	*Gen.*	*Dat.*	*Acc.*	*Abl.*
3rd M/F										

9. Draw a picture of yourself and label it with at least eight *vōcēs*. (But I bet you can get nine.)

Derivative practice

Look for the Latin word in the *vōcēs* that goes with the English derivative. Then look the derivative up in your dictionary.

Latin word	English derivative	What the derivative means
	corpse	
	digit	
	memory	
	vocal	

Probātiō

Vōcēs memorātae
Fill in the definition for each word.

corpus, corporis – 3n – _____

digitus, digitī – 2m – _____

faciēs, faciēī – 5f – _____

lingua, linguae – 1f – _____

manus, manūs – 4f – _____

memoria, memoriae – 1f – _____

oculus, oculī – 2m – _____

pēs, pedis – 3m – _____

vox, vōcis – 3f – _____

vultus, vultūs – 4m – _____

Complete the chart for the 3rd declension M/F.

	Singular					Plural				
	Nom.	Gen.	Dat.	Acc.	Abl.	Nom.	Gen.	Dat.	Acc.	Abl.
3rd M/F										
	* Third declension has lots of possible endings, but ending with an "s" is very common.									

Chapter 12
Review 3

Vōcēs

ars, artis – 3f – skill
auxilium, auxiliī – 2n – help
caelum, caelī – 2n – sky
causa, causae – 1f – cause
cōnsilium, cōnsiliī – 2n – plan
corpus, corporis – 3n – body
digitus, digitī – 2m – finger
dōnum, dōnī – 2n – gift
ecclēsia, ecclēsiae – 1f – church
epistula, epistulae – 1f – letter
equus, equī – 2m – horse
faciēs, faciēī – 5f – face
fōns, fontis – 3m – fountain
fundus, fundī – 2m – farm
lingua, linguae – 1f – tongue
manus, manūs – 4f – hand
memoria, memoriae – 1f –
  memory

negōtium, negōtiī – 2n – business
nihil – n – nothing
oculus, oculī – 2m – eye
oppidum, oppidī – 2n – town
perīculum, perīculī – 2n – danger
pēs, pedis – 3m – foot
portus, portūs – 4m – port
respōnsum, respōnsī – 2n – answer
rūs, rūris – 3n – country(side)
templum, templī – 2n – temple
verbum, verbī – 2n – word
vox, vōcis – 3f – voice
vultus, vultūs – 4m – face

Grammatica Latīna

This unit covered quite a bit of ground. We got both halves of the second declension: masculine and neuter.

	Singular					Plural				
	Nom.	Gen.	Dat.	Acc.	Abl.	Nom.	Gen.	Dat.	Acc.	Abl.
2nd M	-us / -r	-ī	-ō	-um	-ō	-ī	-ōrum	-īs	-ōs	-īs
2nd N	-um	-ī	-ō	-um	-ō	-a	-ōrum	-īs	-a	-īs

We also got half of the 3rd declension, which is tricky and packs two genders into one set of endings. This double duty sounds much harder than it really is. Don't worry about it.

	Singular					Plural				
	Nom.	Gen.	Dat.	Acc.	Abl.	Nom.	Gen.	Dat.	Acc.	Abl.
3rd M/F	*	-is	-ī	-em	-e	-ēs	-um	-ibus	-ēs	-ibus
	* Third declension has lots of possible endings, but ending with an "s" is very common.									

Pēnsa

Vōcēs memorandae
Fill in each blank with the definition supplied in *vōcēs*.

ars, artis – 3f – _____

auxilium, auxiliī – 2n – _____

caelum, caelī – 2n – _____

causa, causae – 1f – _____

cōnsilium, cōnsiliī – 2n – _____

corpus, corporis – 3n – _____

digitus, digitī – 2m – _____

dōnum, dōnī – 2n – _____

ecclēsia, ecclēsiae – 1f – _____

epistula, epistulae – 1f – _____

equus, equī – 2m – _____

faciēs, faciēī – 5f – _____

fōns, fontis – 3m – _____

fundus, fundī – 2m – _____

lingua, linguae – 1f – _____

manus, manūs – 4f – _____

memoria, memoriae – 1f – _____

_____

negōtium, negōtiī – 2n – _____

_____

nihil – n – _____

oculus, oculī – 2m – _____

oppidum, oppidī – 2n – _____

perīculum, perīculī – 2n – _____

pēs, pedis – 3m – _____

portus, portūs – 4m – _____

respōnsum, respōnsī – 2n – _____

rūs, rūris – 3n – _____

templum, templī – 2n – _____

verbum, verbī – 2n – _____

vox, vōcis – 3f – _____

vultus, vultūs – 4m – _____

Derivative practice

Look for the Latin word in the vōcēs that goes with the English derivative. Then look the derivative up in your dictionary.

Latin word	English derivative	What the derivative means
	artificial	
	corporal	
	negotiate	
	verb	

What makes these go together?

Each group of Latin words has another Latin word in common. What is that word?

_____ 1. Epistula, Penna, Verbum   a. Corpus

_____ 2. Digitus, Oculus, Vultus   b. Nihil

_____ 3. Ager, Equus, Fundus   c. Rūs

_____ 4. Negotium, Portus, Templum   d. Aqua

_____ 5. Cōnsilium, Perīculum   e. Scriptor

_____ 6. Fōns, Īnsula, Oceanus   f. Oppidum

Now we're going to do the same thing, but instead of a word that brings it together, we want to find a grammar feature (declension or gender—or maybe both!) that each set of words has in common.

_____ 1. Prīmus, Ultimus   a. feminine

_____ 2. Epistula, Manus, Vox   b. 2nd

_____ 3. Ars, Corpus, Fōns   c. 4th

_____ 4. Caelum, Fundus, Verbum   d. adjective

_____ 5. Manus, Portus, Vultus   e. 3rd

_____ 6. Fōns, Vultus   f. masculine

Chapter 13
Numbers

Vōcēs

ūnus, ūna, ūnum – adj irregular – one
duo, duae, duo – adj irregular – two
trēs, trēs, tria – adj irregular – three
quattuor – adj indeclinable – four
quīnque – adj indeclinable – five
sex – adj indeclinable – six
septem – adj indeclinable – seven
octo – adj indeclinable – eight
novem – adj indeclinable – nine
decem – adj indeclinable – ten

Grammatica Latīna

Let's put down the heavy grammar for a chapter. Instead, we'll learn how to count. One of the things you might have noticed is that the numbers are all adjectives and that numbers four and higher don't decline. (And DO NOT worry about one, two and three, they are irregular.)

If you remember back to other chapters, there are a couple of words that don't decline. *Nihil* and *māne*. So even in normal words, there are some occasional oddballs that don't decline. Lucky you.

Before we head to the *pēnsa*, let's learn how to count with Roman numerals too. It's appropriate, no? Latin numbers were written with Roman numerals after all.

Number	1	2	3	4	5	6	7	8	9	10
Latin number	ūnus	duo	trēs	quattuor	quīnque	sex	septem	octo	novem	decem
Roman numeral	I	II	III	IV	V	VI	VII	VIII	IX	X

If you've never seen Roman numerals before, 4 and 9 are odd. They put a I in front of either V or X—that makes the I subtract. Otherwise, big numerals first, then small. Add it up, and you're there. *Fun hint:* V is half of an X, and there is no zero. (Be glad about that zero thing, it makes multiplicaiton *much* easier.)

Pēnsa

Vōcēs memorandae
Fill in each blank with the word supplied in *vōcēs*. I'll give you definitions.

_____, ____a, ____um – adj irregular – one

_____, ____ae, ____o – adj irregular – two

_____, ____ēs, ____ia – adj irregular – three

_____ – adj indeclinable – four

_____ – adj indeclinable – five

_____ – adj indeclinable – six

_____ – adj indeclinable – seven

_____ – adj indeclinable – eight

_____ – adj indeclinable – nine

_____ – adj indeclinable – ten

Using the vōcēs
Circle the right answer.

1. II + IV = Quīnque Sex

2. IX + I = Novem Decem

3. I + I = Ūnus Duo

4. III + IV = Septem Octo

5. X - II = Septem Octo

6. X - VI = Quattuor Sex

7. IX - IV = Quatuor Quīnque

Fill in the chart with the Roman numerals.

Number	1	2	3	4	5	6	7	8	9	10
Latin number	ūnus	duo	trēs	quattuor	quīnque	sex	septem	octo	novem	decem
Roman numeral										

9. Make a number line from one to ten. Numbers (the words) on top. Numerals (the Is, Vs and Xs) on bottom.

Derivative practice

Look for the Latin word in the *vōcēs* that goes with the English derivative. Then look the derivative up in your dictionary.

Latin word	English derivative	What the derivative means
	unit	
	duet	
	quintet	
	decade	

Probātiō

Vōcēs memoratae
Fill in the definition for each word.
Fill in each blank with the word supplied in *vōcēs*. I'll give you definitions.

_____, _____a, _____um – adj irregular – one

_____, _____ae, _____o – adj irregular – two

_____, _____ēs, _____ia – adj irregular – three

_____ – adj indeclinable – four

_____ – adj indeclinable – five

_____ – adj indeclinable – six

_____ – adj indeclinable – seven

_____ – adj indeclinable – eight

_____ – adj indeclinable – nine

_____ – adj indeclinable – ten

Fill in the chart with the Roman numerals.

Number	1	2	3	4	5	6	7	8	9	10
Latin number	ūnus	duo	trēs	quattuor	quīnque	sex	septem	octo	novem	decem
Roman numeral										

Chapter 14
Verbs

Vōcēs

agit – 3 – s/he does
audit – 4 – s/he hears
dīcit – 3 – s/he says
docet – 2 – s/he teaches
est – LV – s/he is
inquit – irr – s/he says
legit – 3 – s/he reads
ōrat – 1 – s/he prays
rogat – 1 – s/he asks
tacet – 2 – s/he is quiet

Grammatica Latīna

Another easy chapter grammarwise. Sort of. Right now you are learning one specific form of the verb: 3rd person, singular, active, present, indicative. Well, that seems like a lot, doesn't it? The worst part is that it is mostly packed up into one tiny letter.

$$T$$

Made large for effect. Very nice, right? If you look, all of the verbs end with -*t*. That is how you know a verb (for now).

Here's what's tricky.

Ea videt.	*Videt.*
She sees.	(She) sees.

First, take my word for it that *ea* means *she*. The other thing is that in English we need the word *she* or we don't have a sentence. Latin does not even care. No subject? No problem! The verb has it covered. All of the vocabulary words can be their own complete sentence.

The other thing (and we don't care much about it now) is that verbs have a conjugation. It's like declension, but for verbs it's called conjugation. It's important, but not just yet.

Pēnsa

Vōcēs memorandae
Fill in each blank with the definition supplied in *vōcēs*.

agit – 3 – _____

audit – 4 – _____

dīcit – 3 – _____

docet – 2 – _____

est – LV – _____

inquit – irr – _____

legit – 3 – _____

ōrat – 1 – _____

rogat – 1 – _____

tacet – 2 – _____

Using the vōcēs
Circle the right answer.

1. If someone doesn't know something, what might he do? Agit Rogat

2. What word means about the same thing as *dīcit*? Est Inquit

3. If someone is telling you something, what is he doing? Audit Inquit

4. What does a *magister* do? Docet Ōrat

5. If someone is not saying anything, what is he doing? Dīcit Tacet

6. If you are talking to someone, what is he doing? Audit Legit

7. What do you do with a *liber*? Legit Rogat

8. What letter tells you a word is a verb?

A B C D E F G H I J K L M N O P Q R S T U V W X Y Z

9. Draw a picture of yourself doing something and label it with at least six of the *vōcēs* (but if you do two pictures, I bet you can get more).

Derivative practice

Look for the Latin word in the *vōcēs* that goes with the English derivative. Then look the derivative up in your dictionary.

Latin word	English derivative	What the derivative means
	agent	
	doctor	
	auditor	
	tacit	

Probātiō

Vōcēs memorātae

Fill in the definition for each word.

agit – 3 – _____

audit – 4 – _____

dīcit – 3 – _____

docet – 2 – _____

est – LV – _____

inquit – irr – _____

legit – 3 – _____

ōrat – 1 – _____

rogat – 1 – _____

tacet – 2 – _____

What letter tells you a word is a verb?

A B C D E F G H I J K L M N O P Q R S T U V W X Y Z

Vōcēs

cadit – 3 – s/he falls
currit – 3 – s/he runs
dūcit – 3 – s/he leads
fert – irr – s/he carries
it – irr – s/he goes
parat – 1 – s/he prepares
petit – 3 – s/he seeks
sedet – 2 – s/he sits
surgit – 3 – s/he gets up
venit – 4 – s/he comes

Grammatica Latīna

This chapter is almost as complicated as it is going to get here. Really. We're going to make two word sentences. One word will be a noun. Good thing we've already learned a bunch. The other word will be a verb. We now know twenty.

Here are some example sentences.

SN V	V SN
Puer cadit.	*Cadit puer.*
Boy (he) falls.	(He) falls boy.

Hey wait. What's up? For now, don't worry about the SN's and V's. But look at the order of the words. You can put the words in either order? Yes. You can. Let's take another look.

SN V	V SN
Puella currit.	*Currit puella.*
Girl (she) runs.	(She) runs girl.

So what is the lesson here? You can use a noun (in the Nominative case, but we'll worry about that later) and a verb. That is the most basic sentence. Because of the *-t* on the verb and the case on the noun, the word order doesn't matter as much.

Pēnsa

Vōcēs memorandae
Fill in each blank with the definition supplied in *vōcēs*.

cadit – 3 – _____

currit – 3 – _____

dūcit – 3 – _____

fert – irr – _____

it – irr – _____

parat – 1 – _____

petit – 3 – _____

sedet – 2 – _____

surgit – 3 – _____

venit – 4 – _____

Using the vōcēs
Circle the right answer.

1. Someone just tripped. What is she doing? Cadit Dūcit

2. Someone is bringing you something. What is she doing? Fert Surgit

3. Someone is in a chair. What is she doing? It Sedet

4. Someone is in charge. What is she doing? Dūcit Venit

5. Someone is in a marathon. What is she doing? Currit Venit

6. You're waiting for someone. What do you want her to do? Sedet Venit

7. Someone is fixing supper. What is she doing? Cadit Parat

8. Can you put the verb before the subject in Latin? Yes No

Reading very short sentences
Read the sentence in Latin and write its meaning in the blank.

1. Penna cadit.

_____

2. Currit aqua.

_____

3. Soror venit.

_____

4. It vir.

_____

5. Familia est.

_____

Derivative practice
Look for the Latin word in the *vōcēs* that goes with the English derivative. Then look the derivative up in your dictionary.

Latin word	English derivative	What the derivative means
	duke	
	sedentary	
	course	
	dictator	

Probātiō

Vōcēs memorātae
Fill in the definition for each word.

cadit – 3 – _____

currit – 3 – _____

dūcit – 3 – _____

fert – irr – _____

it – irr – _____

parat – 1 – _____

petit – 3 – _____

sedet – 2 – _____

surgit – 3 – _____

venit – 4 – _____

Reading very short sentences
Read the sentence in Latin and write its meaning in the blank.

1. Pater venit.

_____

2. Magistra legit.

_____

3. Rēgina currit.

_____

Chapter 16
Review 4

Vōcēs

ūnus, ūna, ūnum – adj irr – one
duo, duae, duo – adj irr – two
trēs, trēs, tria – adj irr – three
quattuor – adj indec – four
quīnque – adj indec – five
sex – adj indec – six
septem – adj indec – seven
octo – adj indec – eight
novem – adj indec – nine
decem – adj indec – ten
agit – 3 – s/he does
audit – 4 – s/he hears
cadit – 3 – s/he falls
currit – 3 – s/he runs
dīcit – 3 – s/he says

docet – 2 – s/he teaches
dūcit – 3 – s/he leads
est – LV – s/he is
fert – irr – s/he carries
inquit – irr – s/he says
it – irr – s/he goes
legit – 3 – s/he reads
ōrat – 1 – s/he prays
parat – 1 – s/he prepares
petit – 3 – s/he seeks
rogat – 1 – s/he asks
sedet – 2 – s/he sits
surgit – 3 – s/he gets up
tacet – 2 – s/he is quiet
venit – 4 – s/he comes

Grammatica Latīna

Whew! That was an easy unit.

We learned how to count to ten.

Number	1	2	3	4	5	6	7	8	9	10
Latin number	ūnus	duo	trēs	quattuor	quīnque	sex	septem	octo	novem	decem
Roman numeral	I	II	III	IV	V	VI	VII	VIII	IX	X

We learned about verbs. Especially the part with one certain letter.

T

So easy to recognize them! We also know that (for now) all verbs have either *he* or *she* as subjects when there is no subject. So one word can be a sentence!

V
Sedet.
(She) sits.

And that's a little bit different than English. In English you have to say she. Latin doesn't care. We also learned that word order can change. A lot.

SN   V
Fēmina vīvit.
The woman lives.

SN   V
Vīvit fēmina.
The woman lives.

All in all, some things in Latin are really different, but they're not hard.

Pēnsa

Vōcēs memorandae
Fill in each blank with the definition supplied in *vōcēs*.

ūnus, ūna, ūnum – adj irr – _____

duo, duae, duo – adj irr – _____

trēs, trēs, tria – adj irr – _____

quattuor – adj indec – _____

quīnque – adj indec – _____

sex – adj indec – _____

septem – adj indec – _____

octo – adj indec – _____

novem – adj indec – _____

decem – adj indec – _____

agit – 3 – _____

audit – 4 – _____

cadit – 3 – _____

currit – 3 – _____

dīcit – 3 – _____

docet – 2 – _____

dūcit – 3 – _____

est – LV – _____

fert – irr – _____

inquit – irr – _____

it – irr – _____

legit –3 – _____

ōrat – 1 – _____

parat – 1 – _____

petit – 3 – _____

rogat – 1 – _____

sedet – 2 – _____

surgit – 3 – _____

tacet – 2 – _____

venit – 4 – _____

Derivative practice

Look for the Latin word in the *vōcēs* that goes with the English derivative. Then look the derivative up in your dictionary.

Latin word	English derivative	What the derivative means
	legend	
	octave	
	essence	
	voluntary	

What makes these go together?

Each noun goes with a verb. What is that verb?

_____ 1. Dux   a. Sedet

_____ 2. Liber   b. Dūcit

_____ 3. Sella   c. Legit

Fill in the chart with the Roman numerals.

Number	1	2	3	4	5	6	7	8	9	10
Latin number	ūnus	duo	trēs	quattuor	quīnque	sex	septem	octo	novem	decem
Roman numeral										

Reading very short sentences

Read the sentence in Latin and write its meaning in the blank.

1. Dux currit.

_____

2. Rēx tacet.

_____

3. Māter audit.

_____

Chapter 17
3rd Declension N

Vōcēs

carmen, carminis – 3n – song
cūra, cūrae – 1f – care
ludus, ludī – 2m – game
mare, maris – 3In – sea
mundus, mundī – 2m – world
nātūra, nātūrae – 1f – naturee
nōmen, nōminis – 3n – name
pars, partis – 3f – part
quaestiō, quaestiōnis – 3f – question
rēs, reī –5f – thing

Grammatica Latīna

Picking up with the grammar again, we've got another bit of 3rd declension: this time it's neuter.

	Singular					Plural				
	Nom.	Gen.	Dat.	Acc.	Abl.	Nom.	Gen.	Dat.	Acc.	Abl.
3rd N	*	-is	-ī	*	-e	-a	-um	-ibus	-a	-ibus
	* Third declension has lots of possible endings, but ending with an "s" is very common.									

It's kind of a mix between the 2N and 3M/F declensions. Look at everything but Nominative and Accusative. Just like 3rd declension M/F. Look at Nominative and Accusative—they're the same, just like 2N.

Here's an example word declined. Nōmen, to give it a name.

	Nom.	Gen.	Dat.	Acc.	Abl.
Singular	nōmen	nōminis	nōminī	nōmen	nōmine
Plural	nōmina	nōminum	nōminibus	nōmina	nōminibus

Pēnsa

Vōcēs memorandae
Fill in each blank with the definition supplied in *vōcēs*.

carmen, caminis – 3n – _____

cūra, cūrae – 1f – _____

ludus, ludī – 2m – _____

mare, maris – 3If – _____

mundus, mundī – 2m – _____

nātūra, nātūrae – 1f – _____

nōmen, nōminis – 3n – _____

pars, partis – 3f – _____

quaestiō, quaestiōnis – 3f – _____

rēs, reī –5f – _____

Using the vōcēs
Circle the right answer.

1. What do you cut a pie into? Pars Quaestiō

2. If you are carrying a full glass of water, what should you use? Cūra Nōmen

3. What do you have? Nōmen Mundus

4. What is this sentence? Quaestiō Rēs

5. Which one is made of *aqua*? Cūra Mare

6. What is chess? Mare Ludus

7. Where is *nātūra*? Ludus Mundus

8. Complete the chart for the 3rd declension N.

	Singular					Plural				
	Nom.	Gen.	Dat.	Acc.	Abl.	Nom.	Gen.	Dat.	Acc.	Abl.
3rd N										

9. Draw a picture and label it with six of the *vōces*. (But you could probably get to eight without too much trouble).

Derivative practice

Look for the Latin word in the *vōcēs* that goes with the English derivative. Then look the derivative up in your dictionary.

Latin word	English derivative	What the derivative means
	cure	
	marine	
	Nominative	
	question	

Probātiō

Vōcēs memorātae
Fill in the definition for each word.

carmen, caminis – 3n – _____

cūra, cūrae – 1f – _____

ludus, ludī – 2m – _____

mare, maris – 3If – _____

mundus, mundī – 2m – _____

nātūra, nātūrae – 1f – _____

nōmen, nōminis – 3n – _____

pars, partis – 3f – _____

quaestiō, quaestiōnis – 3f – _____

rēs, reī –5f – _____

Complete the chart for the 3rd declension neuter.

	Singular					Plural				
	Nom.	Gen.	Dat.	Acc.	Abl.	Nom.	Gen.	Dat.	Acc.	Abl.
3rd N										

Vōcēs

cīvitās, cīvitātis – 3f – citizenship
cōnsul, cōnsulis – 3m – consul (Roman political leader)
gēns, gentis – 3f – tribe
imperium, imperiī – 2n – empire
latīnus, latīna, latīnum – adj – Latin
nātus, nātūs – 4m – birth
populus, populī – 2m – people
Rōma, Rōmae – 1f – Rome
Rōmānus, Rōmāna, Rōmānum – adj – Roman
Senātus, Senātūs – 4m – Senate

Grammatica Latīna

The poor 4th declension. It's small and looks confusingly like the 2nd declension M. It's so bad that you've got to watch the macrons!

The good news is that the forms are all pretty obvious when U pick up on the U. Aside from all the U U will see, all of the words in this declension are masculine. Expect for *manus, manūs* (hand). It's feminine.

	Singular					Plural				
	Nom.	Gen.	Dat.	Acc.	Abl.	Nom.	Gen.	Dat.	Acc.	Abl.
4th M	-us	-ūs	-uī	-um	-ū	-ūs	-uum	-ibus	-ūs	-ibus

And as always, an example word in all the cases for the declension.

	Nom.	Gen.	Dat.	Acc.	Abl.
Singular	nātus	nātūs	nātuī	nātum	nātū
Plural	nātūs	nātuum	nātibus	nātūs	nātibus

There is also a 4th declension N, but we won't worry about it. It's extremely uncommon and has maybe 3 words in it.

Pēnsa

Vōcēs memorandae
Fill in each blank with the definition supplied in *vōcēs*.

cīvitās, cīvitātis – 3f – _____

cōnsul, cōnsulis – 3m – _____

gēns, gentis – 3f – _____

imperium, imperiī – 2n – _____

latīnus, latīna, latīnum – adj – _____

nātus, nātūs – 4m – _____

populus, populī – 2m – _____

Rōma, Rōmae – 1f – _____

Rōmānus, Rōmāna, Rōmānum – adj – _____

Senātus, Senātūs – 4m – _____

Using the vōcēs
Circle the right answer.

1. Who is *Rōmānus*? Aqua Cōnsul

2. What can you find in Ancient Rome and Washinton, D.C.? Cōnsul Senātus

3. What just happened to a baby? Imperium Nātus

4. What word better describes a *gēns*? Populus Rōma

5. What word better describes an *imperium*? Latīnum Rōmānum

6. If your friend is from Rōma, what is she? Rōmāna Senātus

7. What is a big group of *vir* and *fēmina*? Cōnsul Populus

8. Complete the chart for the 4th declension M.

	Singular					Plural				
	Nom.	Gen.	Dat.	Acc.	Abl.	Nom.	Gen.	Dat.	Acc.	Abl.
4th M										

9. Draw a picture of ancient Roman and label it with at least six *vōcēs*. (Some of these are tricky to draw.)

Derivative practice

Look for the Latin word in the *vōcēs* that goes with the English derivative. Then look the derivative up in your dictionary.

Latin word	English derivative	What the derivative means
	city	
	imperial	
	native	
	senator	

Probātiō

Vōcēs memorātae
Fill in the definition for each word.

cīvitās, cīvitātis – 3f – _____

cōnsul, cōnsulis – 3m – _____

gēns, gentis – 3f – _____

imperium, imperiī – 2n – _____

latīnus, latīna, latīnum – adj – _____

nātus, nātūs – 4m – _____

populus, populī – 2m – _____

Rōma, Rōmae – 1f – _____

Rōmānus, Rōmāna, Rōmānum – adj – _____

Senātus, Senātūs – 4m – _____

Complete the chart for the 4th declension masculine.

	Singular					Plural				
	Nom.	Gen.	Dat.	Acc.	Abl.	Nom.	Gen.	Dat.	Acc.	Abl.
4th M										

Chapter 19
5th Declension

Vōcēs

amor, amōris – 3m – love

animus, animī – 2m – soul, mind

deus, deī – 2m – god

dominus, dominī – 2m – lord

fidēs, fideī – 5f –faith

glōria, glōriae – 1f – glory

munus, muneris – 3n – job, gift

pecūnia, pecūniae – 1f – money

rēgnum, rēgnī – 2n – kingdom

spīritus, spīritūs – 4m – spirit

Grammatica Latīna

At last, the last declension. Most of the words in the 5th declension are feminine, and *diēs, dieī – 5m – day* is the exception to show the rule (as well as *meridiēs*, a compound of *diēs*). In some ways the 5th declension is kind of like the 1st declension—look at the singular. But it is also like the 3rd declension m/f—look at the plural.

	Singular					Plural				
	Nom.	Gen.	Dat.	Acc.	Abl.	Nom.	Gen.	Dat.	Acc.	Abl.
5th	-ēs	-eī	-eī	-em	-ē	-ēs	-ērum	-ēbus	-ēs	-ēbus

Like the 1st, 2nd M, 2nd N and 4th M, the 5th declension is nice and regular. (Why do you hurt our memories, 3rd declension? Why?) Here is *fidēs* put through all of its cases.

	Nom.	Gen.	Dat.	Acc.	Abl.
Singular	fidēs	fideī	fideī	fidem	fidē
Plural	fidēs	fidērum	fidēbus	fidēs	fidēbus

Pēnsa

Vōcēs memorandae

Fill in each blank with the definition supplied in *vōcēs*.

amor, amōris – 3m – _____

animus, animī – 2m – _____

deus, deī – 2m – _____

dominus, dominī – 2m – _____

fidēs, fideī – 5f – _____

glōria, glōriae – 1f – _____

munus, muneris – 3n – _____

pecūnia, pecūniae – 1f – _____

rēgnum, rēgnī – 2n – _____

spīritus, spīritūs – 4m – _____

Using the *vōcēs*

Circle the right answer.

1. What can you get *pecūnia* for doing? Fidēs Munus

2. If you believe in God, what do you have? Fidēs Pecūnia

3. *Animus* has a synonym. Which? Rēgnum Spīritus

4. Which one belongs to a *rēx* or *rēgīna*? Amor Rēgnum

5. What word better describes a dollar? Fidēs Pecūnia

6. Which one might a *mīles* have? Glōria Spīritus

7. Who has a *rēgnum*? Dominus Glōria

8. Complete the chart for the 5th declension.

	Singular					Plural				
	Nom.	Gen.	Dat.	Acc.	Abl.	Nom.	Gen.	Dat.	Acc.	Abl.
5th										

74

9. Draw a picture and label it with at least six *vōcēs*. (Some of these are tricky to draw.)

Derivative practice

Look for the Latin word in the *vōcēs* that goes with the English derivative. Then look the derivative up in your dictionary.

Latin word	English derivative	What the derivative means
	animated	
	dominate	
	munificent	
	spiritual	

Probātiō

Vōcēs memorātae
Fill in the definition for each word.

amor, amōris – 3m – _____

animus, animī – 2m – _____

deus, deī – 2m – _____

dominus, dominī – 2m – _____

fidēs, fideī – 5f – _____

glōria, glōriae – 1f – _____

munus, muneris – 3n – _____

pecūnia, pecūniae – 1f – _____

rēgnum, rēgnī – 2n – _____

spīritus, spīritūs – 4m – _____

Complete the chart for the 5th declension.

	Singular					Plural				
	Nom.	Gen.	Dat.	Acc.	Abl.	Nom.	Gen.	Dat.	Acc.	Abl.
5th										

Vōcēs

amor, amōris – 3m – love

animus, animī – 2m – soul, mind

carmen, carminis – 3n – song

cīvitās, cīvitātis – 3f – citizenship

cōnsul, cōnsulis – 3m – consul (Roman political leader)

cūra, cūrae – 1f – care

deus, deī – 2m – god

dominus, dominī – 2m – lord

fidēs, fideī – 5f –faith

gēns, gentis – 3f – tribe

glōria, glōriae – 1f – glory

imperium, imperiī – 2n – empire

latīnus, latīna, latīnum – adj – Latin

ludus, ludī – 2m – game

mare, maris – 3In – sea

mundus, mundī – 2m – world

munus, muneris – 3n – job, gift

nātūra, nātūrae – 1f – nature

nātus, nātūs – 4m – birth

nōmen, nōminis – 3n – name

pars, partis – 3f – part

pecūnia, pecūniae – 1f – money

populus, populī – 2m – people

quaestiō, quaestiōnis – 3f – question

rēgnum, rēgnī – 2n – kingdom

rēs, reī –5f – thing

Rōma, Rōmae – 1f – Rome

Rōmānus, Rōmāna, Rōmānum – adj – Roman

Senātus, Senātūs – 4m – Senate

spīritus, spīritūs – 4m – spirit

Grammatica Latīna

That was an easy unit. We covered the 3rd declension Neuter.

	Singular					Plural				
	Nom.	Gen.	Dat.	Acc.	Abl.	Nom.	Gen.	Dat.	Acc.	Abl.
3rd N	*	-is	-ī	*	-e	-a	-um	-ibus	-a	-ibus
	* Third declension has lots of possible endings, but ending with an "s" is very common.									

And the 4th declension, which is mostly masculine.

	Singular					Plural				
	Nom.	Gen.	Dat.	Acc.	Abl.	Nom.	Gen.	Dat.	Acc.	Abl.
4th M	-us	-ūs	-uī	-um	-ū	-ūs	-uum	-ibus	-ūs	-ibus

And the 5th declension, which is mostly feminine.

	Singular					Plural				
	Nom.	Gen.	Dat.	Acc.	Abl.	Nom.	Gen.	Dat.	Acc.	Abl.
5th	-ēs	-eī	-eī	-em	-ē	-ēs	-ērum	-ēbus	-ēs	-ēbus

With these three groups, you've learned all the noun endings we're going to cover in this book.

Pēnsa

Vōcēs memorandae
Fill in each blank with the definition supplied in *vōcēs*.

amor, amōris – 3m – _____

animus, animī – 2m – _____

carmen, carminis – 2n – _____

cīvitās, cīvitātis – 3f – _____

_____

cōnsul, cōnsulis – 3m – _____

cūra, cūrae – 1f – _____

deus, deī – 2m – _____

dominus, dominī – 2m – _____

fidēs, fideī – 5f – _____

gēns, gentis – 3f – _____

glōria, glōriae – 1f – _____

imperium, imperiī – 2n – _____

_____

latīnus, latīna, latīnum – adj – _____

_____

ludus, ludī – 2m – _____

mare, maris – 3In – _____

mundus, mundī – 2m – _____

munus, muneris – 3n – _____

nātūra, nātūrae – 1m – _____

nātus, nātūs – 4m – _____

nōmen, nōminis – 3n – _____

pars, partis – 3f – _____

pecūnia, pecūniae – 1f – _____

populus, populī – 2m – _____

quaestiō, quaestiōnis – 3f – _____

rēgnum, rēgnī – 2n – _____

rēs, reī – 5f – _____

Rōma, Rōmae – 1f – _____

Rōmānus, Rōmāna, Rōmānum – adj – _

_____

Senātus, Senātūs – 4m – _____

spiritus, spiritūs – 4m – _____

Derivative practice

Look for the Latin word in the vōcēs that goes with the English derivative. Then look the derivative up in your dictionary.

Latin word	English derivative	What the derivative means
	empire	
	fidelity	
	mundane	
	partial	

Fill in the chart with the Roman numerals.

	Singular					Plural				
	Nom.	*Gen.*	*Dat.*	*Acc.*	*Abl.*	*Nom.*	*Gen.*	*Dat.*	*Acc.*	*Abl.*
3rd N										
4th M										
5th										
	* Third declension has lots of possible endings, but ending with an "s" is very common.									

Reading very short sentences

Read the sentence in Latin and write its meaning in the blank.

1. Cōnsul dūcit.

_____

2. Gēns it.

_____

3. Deus surgit.

_____

Chapter 21
Labels

Vōcēs

amīca, amīcae – 1f – friend (girl, woman)
amīcus, amīcī – 2m –friend (boy, man)
fīlia, fīliae – 1f – daughter
fīlius, fīliī – 2m – son
homo, hominis – 3m – human
nōn – adv – not
nuntius, nuntiī – 2m – messenger
rosa, rosae – 1f – rose
spina, spinae – 1f – thorn
vīta, vītae – 1f – life

Grammatica Latīna

You may have noticed some letters above the words in the example sentences in chapter 15 (p. 57). What are they doing there? Their purpose is to show you what each word is doing in terms of grammar rather than telling you what they mean. Think of it as a road map telling you how to get to knowing what the sentence means. We will use very few labels in this book. Here they are.

Label	Stands for	Other info
SN	Subject (Noun)	Optional in Latin.
DO	Direct Object	Some verbs need a DO, some don't.
LV	Linking Verb	We'll learn about this in chapter 22.
V	(Intransitive) Verb	This verb doesn't need a DO.
Vt	Verb, transitive	This verb usually wants a DO.
PrN	Predicate Noun	A noun that comes after an LV.
PrA	Predicate Adjective	An adjective that comes after an LV.
Adj	Adjective	Modifies a noun.
Adv	Adverb	Modifies V and Adj.
C	Conjunction	Joins things together.

Pēnsa

Vōcēs memorandae
Fill in each blank with the definition supplied in *vōcēs*.

amīca, amīcae – 1f – _____

amīcus, amīcī – 2m – _____

fīlia, fīliae – 1f – _____

fīlius, fīliī – 2m – _____

homo, hominis – 3m – _____

nōn – adv – _____

nuntius, nuntiī – 2m – _____

rosa, rosae – 1f – _____

spina, spinae – 1f – _____

vīta, vītae – 1f – _____

Using the vōcēs
Circle the right answer.

1. What does a *rosa* have? Nuntius Spina

2. Which one better describes *fīlia*? Homo Nōn

3. If you want to reverse a sentence's meaning, which do you want? Fīlius Nōn

4. Which one can be a *puella*? Fīlia Fīlius

5. Which one can be a *puer*? Fīlia Fīlius

6. Who is your friend? Amīca Spina

7. Which one has *vīta*? Homo Nōn

8. Which labels could apply to *rosa*?

    SN   DO   LV   V   Vt   PrN   PrA   Adj   Adv   C

9. Draw a picture and label it with at least seven *vōcēs*.

Derivative practice

Look for the Latin word in the *vōcēs* that goes with the English derivative. Then look the derivative up in your dictionary.

Latin word	English derivative	What the derivative means
	amicable	
	filial	
	spine	
	vital	

Probātiō

Vōcēs memorātae

Fill in the definition for each word.

amīca, amīcae – 1f – _____

amīcus, amīcī – 2m – _____

fīlia, fīliae – 1f – _____

fīlius, fīliī – 2m – _____

homo, hominis – 3m – _____

nōn – adv – _____

nuntius, nuntiī – 2m – _____

rosa, rosae – 1f – _____

spina, spinae – 1f – _____

vīta, vītae – 1f – _____

Which labels could apply to a verb?

SN   DO   LV   V   Vt   PrN   PrA   Adj   Adv   C

Chapter 22
The Linking Verb

Vōcēs

aeger, aegra, aegrum – adj – sick
astūtus, astūta, astūtum – adj – clever
carus, cara, carum – adj – dear
lentus, lenta, lentum – adj – slow
magnus, magna, magnum – adj – big, great
meus, mea, meum – adj – my, mine
noster, nostra, nostrum – adj – our, ours
pulcher, pulchra, pulchrum – adj – beautiful
tuus, tua, tuum – adj – your, yours
vester, vestra, vestrum – adj – your, yours (pl)

Grammatica Latīna

There's one really important verb. It is *est*. It is so important that it gets its own special label: LV. It also has its own special grammar. There are pretty much two combinations that can happen. LV with a noun (PrN), LV with an adjective (PrA).

SN LV   PRA
Sōl est pulcher.
The sun is beautiful.

ADJ LV   PRN
Astūta est soror.
The sister is clever.

SN   LV   PRN
Pater est parēns.
Father is a parent.

SN   LV   PRA
Fēmina est aegra.
The woman is sick.

Now, in English we really care which one is the SN and which one is the PrN/PrA. It affects the word order. Latin doesn't really care. So, anything that comes before the LV is Adj or SN. Anything that comes after is PrA or PrN. These may or may not be accurate to how it sounds best in English. But you saw that in the examples, right?

Pēnsa

Vōcēs memorandae

Fill in each blank with the definition supplied in *vōcēs*.

aeger, aegra, aegrum – adj – _____

astūtus, astūta, astūtum – adj – _____

carus, cara, carum – adj – _____

lentus, lenta, lentum – adj – _____

magnus, magna, magnum – adj – _____

meus, mea, meum – adj _____

noster, nostra, nostrum – adj – _____

pulcher, pulchra, pulchrum – adj – _____

tuus, tua, tuum – adj – _____

vester, vestra, vestrum – adj – _____

Using the vōcēs

Circle the right answer.

1. Which one is mine? Meus Noster

2. Which one describes someone with a fever? Aeger Astūtus

3. Which one describes something we share? Noster Vester

4. Which one describes a really nice sunset? Graecus Pulcher

5. Which one belongs to the two of you? Tuus Vester

6. Which word describes something big? Lentus Magnus

7. Which word describes something very close to your heart? Carus Vester

8. What comes before the LV? SN/ADJ PrN/PrA

Labeling very short sentences

Read the sentence in Latin and label it with SN, ADJ, PrN or PrA. I'll take care of the LV for you.

              LV
1. Respōnsum est astūtum.

             LV
2. Nostra est ecclēsia.

              LV
3. Negōtium est vestrum.

            LV
4. Digitus est lentus.

           LV
5. Vox est epistula.

Derivative practice

Look for the Latin word in the *vōcēs* that goes with the English derivative. Then look the derivative up in your dictionary.

Latin word	English derivative	What the derivative means
	astute	
	magnitude	
	magnify	
	pulchritude	

Probātiō

Vōcēs memorātae

Fill in the definition for each word.

aeger, aegra, aegrum – adj – _____

astūtus, astūta, astūtum – adj – _____

carus, cara, carum – adj – _____

lentus, lenta, lentum – adj – _____

magnus, magna, magnum – adj – _____

meus, mea, meum – adj _____

noster, nostra, nostrum – adj – _____

pulcher, pulchra, pulchrum – adj – _____

tuus, tua, tuum – adj – _____

vester, vestra, vestrum – adj – _____

Circle the LV in each of the following sentences.

1. Ecclēsia est nostra.

2. Negōtium vestrum est.

3. Est digitus lentus.

Chapter 23
Intransitive Verbs

Vōcēs

amat – 1 – s/he loves
cognōscit – 3 – s/he knows
horrēscit – 3 – s/he gets scared
-ne – ? – asks yes/no question
nescit – 4 – s/he does not know
putat – 1 – s/he thinks
spectat – 1 – s/he looks at
timet – 2 – s/he fears
videt – 2 – s/he sees
vīvit – 4 – s/he lives

Grammatica Latīna

Now for a much larger group of verbs. We give them the big name intransitive. This name is secret grammar code for verbs that do not have a direct object. We label them V. Here is an example of an intransitive verb in action.

SN   V
Puer vīvit.
The boy lives.

SN   V
Vir nescit.
The man doesn't know.

Really, not much to it. Is there?

That *-ne* thing is a different story. It asks yes/no questions and attaches to the first word in the sentence. Like this.

SN ? V
Puerne vīvit?
Does the boy live?

V ? SN
Nescitne vir?
Does the man not know?

It's a little strange, but it's not too different from how English adds a *does* to questions like that.

Pēnsa

Vōcēs memorandae
Fill in each blank with the definition supplied in *vōcēs*.

amat – 4 – _____

cognōscit – 3 – _____

horrēscit – 3 – _____

-ne – ? – _____

nescit – 4 – _____

putat – 1 – _____

spectat – 1 – _____

timet – 2 – _____

videt – 2 – _____

vīvit – 4 – _____

Using the vōcēs
Circle the right answer.

1. If someone has already met your friend, what are they doing? Cognōscit Pōnit

2. How would you ask a question? Amat -ne

3. Which word can mean the opposite of *nescit*? Cognōscit Timet

4. If someone doesn't give a *respōnsum*, what might be happening? Nescit Timet

5. If someone is coming up with a *respōnsum*, what are they doing? Putat Spectat

6. What word means about the same thing as *timet*? Amat Horrēscit

7. What do you do at a movie? Nescit Videt

8. To make a question out of a sentence, which word do you put *-ne* on the end of?
    First   Second   Anywhere   Last

Reading very short sentences

Read the sentence in Latin and write its meaning in the blank.

1. Magistra horrēscit.

_____

2. Equus vīvit.

_____

3. Pater nescit.

_____

4. Māter sedet.

_____

5. Fīlia putat.

_____

Derivative practice

Look for the Latin word in the *vōcēs* that goes with the English derivative. Then look the derivative up in your dictionary.

Latin word	English derivative	What the derivative means
	horrify	
	deposit	
	spectator	
	vivid	

Probātiō

Vōcēs memorātae

Fill in the definition for each word.

amat – 4 – _____

cognōscit – 3 – _____

horrēscit – 3 – _____

-ne – ? – _____

nescit – 4 – _____

putat – 1 – _____

spectat – 1 – _____

timet – 2 – _____

videt – 2 – _____

vīvit – 4 – _____

Label the following sentences.

1. Equus surgit.

2. Sedet māter.

3. Vīvitne pater?

Vōcēs

aeger, aegra, aegrum – adj – sick

amat – 1 – s/he loves

amīca, amīcae – 1f – friend (girl, woman)

amīcus, amīcī – 2m –friend (boy, man)

astūtus, astūta, astūtum – adj – clever

carus, cara, carum – adj – dear

cognōscit – 3 – s/he knows

fīlia, fīliae – 1f – daughter

fīlius, fīliī – 2m – son

homo, hominis – 3m – human

horrēscit – 3 – s/he gets scared

lentus, lenta, lentum – adj – slow

magnus, magna, magnum – adj – big, great

meus, mea, meum – adj – my, mine

-ne – ? – asks yes/no question

nescit – 4 – s/he does not know

nōn – adv – not

noster, nostra, nostrum – adj – our, ours

nuntius, nuntiī – 2m – messenger

pulcher, pulchra, pulchrum – adj – beautiful

putat – 1 – s/he thinks

rosa, rosae – 1f – rose

spectat – 1 – s/he looks at

spina, spinae – 1f – thorn

timet – 2 – s/he fears

tuus, tua, tuum – adj – your, yours

vester, vestra, vestrum – adj – your, yours (pl)

videt – 2 – s/he sees

vīta, vītae – 1f – life

vīvit – 4 – s/he lives

Grammatica Latīna

In this unit we learned a whole bunch of labels.

Label	Stands for	Other info
SN	Subject (Noun)	Optional in Latin.
DO	Direct Object	Some verbs need a DO, some don't.
LV	Linking Verb	We'll learn about this in chapter 22.
V	(Intransitive) Verb	This verb doesn't need a DO.
Vt	Verb, transitive	This verb usually wants a DO.
PrN	Predicate Noun	A noun that comes after an LV.
PrA	Predicate Adjective	An adjective that comes after an LV.
Adj	Adjective	Modifies a noun.
Adv	Adverb	Modifies V and Adj.
C	Conjunction	Joins things together.

The cool thing is that we also learned how to put some of those labels to use. In the case of the LV, we know how to use SN, ADJ, PrN and PrA.

SN LV   PRA
Sōl est pulcher.
The sun is beautiful.

ADJ LV   PRN
Callida est soror.
The sister is clever.

This type of sentence is really common in Latin, so it's good to keep it in mind. We also learned about sentences with intransitive verbs.

SN   V
Puer surgit.
The boy gets up.

SN   V
Vir nescit.
The man doesn't know.

Pēnsa

Vōcēs memorandae
Fill in each blank with the definition supplied in *vōcēs*.

aeger, aegra, aegrum – adj – _____

amat – 1 – _____

amīca, amīcae – 1f – _____

amīcus, amīcī – 2m – _____

astūtus, astūta, astūtum – adj – _____
_____

carus, cara, carum – adj – _____

cognōscit – 3 – _____

fīlia, fīliae – 1f – _____

fīlius, fīliī – 2m – _____

homo, hominis – 3m – _____

horrēscit – 3 – _____

lentus, lenta, lentum – adj – _____

magnus, magna, magnum – adj – _____
_____

meus, mea, meum – adj – _____

-ne – ? – _____

nescit – 4 – _____

nōn – adv – _____

noster, nostra, nostrum – adj – _____

nuntius, nuntiī – 2m – _____

pulcher, pulchra, pulchrum – adj – _____
_____

putat – 1 – _____

rosa, rosae – 1f – _____

spectat – 1 – _____

spina, spinae – 1f – _____

timet – 2 – _____

tuus, tua, tuum – adj – _____

vester, vestra, vestrum – adj – _____
_____

videt – 2 – _____

vīta, vītae – 1f – _____

vīvit – 4 – _____

Derivative practice

Look for the Latin word in the *vōcēs* that goes with the English derivative. Then look the derivative up in your dictionary.

Latin word	English derivative	What the derivative means
	orator	
	posit	
	acute	
	civic	

What makes these go together?

Each group of Latin words has another Latin word in common. What is that word?

_____ 1. Vir, Fēmina, Puer   a. Oculus

_____ 2. Fīlius, Fīliae, Carus   b. Vīta

_____ 3. Nuntius, Amīca, Respōnsum   c. Familia

_____ 4. Vīvit, Corpus   d. Homo

_____ 5. Spectat, Videt   e. Magister

_____ 6. Doctus, Dūcit, Schola   f. Epistula

Reading very short sentences

Read each sentence in Latin and label it.

1. Amīca est vestra.

2. Amīcus nescit.

3. Surgit homo.

Chapter 25
Accusative Case

Vōcēs

casus, casūs – 4m – case
exemplum, exemplī – 2n – example
forma, formae – 1f – shape
genus, generis – 3f – gender
grammatica, grammaticae – 1f – grammar
nōmen, nōminis – 3n – noun
numerus, numerī – 2m – number
professor, professōris – 3m – professor
rhētorica, rhētoricae – 1f – rhetoric
studium, studiī – 2n – study

Grammatica Latīna

So way back in chapter 6 we learned the names of the cases, but didn't bother with them much past that. We are now going to learn how to make our Nominative-Genetive noun pairs into Accusative case. For the most part it will be easy. Take the Nominative noun, get rid of the ending and add the Accusative ending from the same declension.

Accusative	Sing.
1st	-am
2nd M	-um
2nd N	-um
3rd M/F	-em
3rd N	-*
4th	-um
5th	-em

fīlia ☞ fīli__ ☞ fīliam

manus ☞ man__ ☞ manum

Easy. Except for the 3rd declension (and those 2nd Declension M words that end with -r). Because you aren't really lopping off the Nominative. You're lopping off the Genitive—it's more important to start with. It really works like this.

professōris ☞ professōr__ ☞ professōrem (yes, the macron)

librī ☞ libr__ ☞ librum

generis ☞ gener__ ☞ generem

It's not at all tricky, but it does take some getting used to. So why bother with this mess? It is how we get the Direct Object (DO).

97

Pēnsa

Vōcēs memorandae
Fill in each blank with the definition supplied in *vōcēs*.

casus, casūs – 4m – _____

exemplum, exemplī – 2n – _____

forma, formae – 1f – _____

genus, generis – 3f – _____

grammatica, grammaticae – 1f – _____

nōmen, nōminis – 3n – _____

numerus, numerī – 2m – _____

professor, professōris – 3m – _____

rhētorica, rhētoricae – 1f – _____

studium, studiī – 2n – _____

Using the vōcēs
Circle the right answer.

1. Which one does a nōmen have? Casus Studium

2. Which one has numerus? Genus Nōmen

3. Which one might an orator want to know? Exemplum Rhētorica

4. Who teaches a class? Grammatica Professor

5. Which one can be a synonym for triangle? Forma Nōmen

6. Masculine, Feminine and Neuter? Genus Numerus

7. Which one is a part of language? Grammatica Studium

8. Which is more important for making the Accusative case? Nominative Genitive

Making nouns Accusative

Now it's your turn. Make each of the nouns listed below into their Accusative forms. (Remember that we are using the Genitive form!)

Genitive case	No ending	Accusative ending
ex. generis ☞	gener__ ☞	*generem*
1. casūs ☞	cas__ ☞	
2. formae ☞	form__ ☞	
3. professōris ☞	professōr__ ☞	
4. numerī ☞	numer__ ☞	
5. studiī ☞	studi__ ☞	

Derivative practice

Look for the Latin word in the *vōcēs* that goes with the English derivative. Then look the derivative up in your dictionary.

Latin word	English derivative	What the derivative means
	e.g.	
	formal	
	generic	
	Nominative	

Probātiō

Vōcēs memorātae

Fill in the definition for each word.

casus, casūs – 4m – _____

exemplum, exemplī – 2n – _____

forma, formae – 1f – _____

genus, generis – 3f – _____

grammatica, grammaticae – 1f – _____

nōmen, nōminis – 3n – _____

numerus, numerī – 2m – _____

professor, professōris – 3m – _____

rhētorica, rhētoricae – 1f – _____

studium, studiī – 2n – _____

Mark the nouns that aren't Accusative.

_____ 1. Generī

_____ 2. Professōrem

_____ 3. Exemplum

_____ 4. Casuī

_____ 5. Grammaticam

Chapter 26
Transitive Verbs

Vōcēs

aperit – 4 – s/he opens
dat – 1 – s/he gives
facit –3io – s/he makes
habet – 2 – s/he has
invenit – 4 – s/he finds
mittit – 3 – s/he sends
ostendit – 3 – s/he holds out
pōnit – 3 – s/he places
significat – 1 – s/he means, it means
vult – irr – s/he wants

Grammatica Latīna

In the last chapter we learned how to make Accusative case from nouns so that we could get to this chapter. It is about transitive verbs. Transitive is special grammar talk for a kind of verb that needs a direct object.

We've seen these sorts of sentences before in chapter 15, so this isn't some great news. But to review, here is how it works. Notice each sentence has three elements. One subject—SN. One verb—Vt. One direct object—DO.

SN   VT   DO
Magister petit librum.
The teacher seeks the book.

SN   DO   VT
Fīlia patrem spectat.
The daughter looks at father.

Except that we know a secret about the subject. We can get rid of it and let the -t on the verb do the work.

VT   DO
Petit librum.
He seeks the book.

DO   VT
Patrem spectat.
She looks at father.

What could be easier?

Pēnsa

Vōcēs memorandae
Fill in each blank with the definition supplied in *vōcēs*.

aperit – 4 – _____

dat – 1 – _____

facit –3io – _____

habet – 2 – _____

invenit – 4 – _____

mittit – 3 – _____

ostendit – 3 – _____

pōnit – 3 – _____

significat – 1 – _____

vult – irr – _____

Using the vōcēs
Circle the right answer.

1. If someone is not hiding in hide and seek, what are they doing? Facit Petit

2. Something is missing. What is someone doing? Habet Vult

3. What would someone do with an *epistula*? Mittit Significat

4. What would someone do with a *dōnum*? Dat Significat

5. If someone is building something, what are they doing? Facit Invenit

6. Someone is opening a door. What are they doing? Aperit Pōnit

7. Someone has something heavy. What could they do? Pōnit Significat

8. What does a transitive sentence have that others don't? SN DO Vt

Reading very short sentences

Read the sentence in Latin and write its meaning in the blank.

1. Professor puellam docet.

_____

2. Fēmina equum petit.

_____

3. Deus facit rosam.

_____

4. Rosa spinam habet.

_____

5. Vir spinam invenit.

_____

Derivative practice

Look for the Latin word in the _vōcēs_ that goes with the English derivative. Then look the derivative up in your dictionary.

Latin word	English derivative	What the derivative means
	apterture	
	Dative	
	inventor	
	signify	

Probātiō

Vōcēs memorātae
Fill in the definition for each word.

aperit – 4 – _____

dat – 1 – _____

facit –3io – _____

habet – 2 – _____

invenit – 4 – _____

mittit – 3 – _____

ostendit – 3 – _____

pōnit – 3 – _____

significat – 1 – _____

vult – irr – _____

1. What does a transitive sentence have that others don't? SN DO Vt

Vōcēs

cūr – adv – why?

nōnne – adv – asks question expecting yes answer

quālis – adj (special) – what kind?

quandō – adv – when?

quid – pronoun – what?

quis – pronoun – who?

quō – adv – where to?

quōmodo – adv – how?

quot – adv – how many?

ubi – adv – where?

Grammatica Latīna

What good would it be if you couldn't ask questions? The rules for making questions in Latin are pretty easy. The extra easy part is that most of the question words begin with QU-. Ok, ready for the rule?

You put the question word first in the question.

ADV LV PRN
Ubi est Rōma?
Where is Rome?

SN LV PRN
Quis est magistra?
Who is the teacher?

SN LV PRN
Quid est rosa?
What is a rose?

ADJ LV PRN
Quālis est discipula?
What kind of student is she?

Isn't that easy? You know what the hard part is? Answering questions.

Pēnsa

Vōcēs memorandae
Fill in each blank with the definition supplied in *vōcēs*.

cūr – adv – _____

nōnne – adv – _____

quālis – adj (special) – _____

quandō – adv – _____

quid – pronoun – _____

quis – pronoun – _____

quō – adv – _____

quōmodo – adv – _____

quot – adv – how _____

ubi – adv – _____

Using the vōcēs
Circle the right question.

1. Cūr? Ubi?   In the kitchen.

2. Quandō? Quō?   To grandma's house.

3. Quis? Quālis?   Colonel Mustard.

4. Nōnne? Quōmodo?   Yes.

5. Quot? Ubi?   Decem.

6. Nōnne? Quōmodo?   With the rope.

7. Cūr? Quandō?   At ten.

8. Where do question words (almost always) go in a Latin sentence?
      First   Second   Anywhere   Last

Reading very short sentences
Read the sentence in Latin and label them.

1. Quōmodo magistra discipulum docet?

2. Cūr puer facit sellam?

3. Quālis est sella?

4. Ubi fēmina sedet?

5. Quando magister scholam dūcit?

Derivative practice
These words don't really apply to deriviatives very well. So, skip the derivatives section for this chapter.

Probātiō

Vōcēs memorātae
Fill in the definition for each word.

cūr – adv – _____

nōnne – adv – _____

quālis – adj (special) – _____

quandō – adv – _____

quid – pronoun – _____

quis – pronoun – _____

quō – adv – _____

quōmodo – adv – _____

quot – adv – how _____

ubi – adv – _____

Vōcēs

aperit – 4 – s/he opens

casus, casūs – 4m – case

cūr – adv – why?

dat – 1 – s/he gives

exemplum, exemplī – 2n – example

facit –3io – s/he makes

forma, formae – 1f – shape

genus, generis – 3f – gender

grammatica, grammaticae – 1f – grammar

habet – 2 – s/he has

invenit – 4 – s/he finds

mittit – 3 – s/he sends

nōmen, nōminis – 3n – noun

nōnne – adv – asks question expecting yes answer

numerus, numerī – 2m – number

ostendit – 3 – s/he holds out

pōnit – 3 – s/he places

professor, professōris – 3m – professor

quālis – adj (special) – what kind?

quandō – adv – when?

quid – pronoun – what?

quis – pronoun – who?

quō – adv – where to?

quōmodo – adv – how?

quot – adv – how many?

rhētorica, rhētoricae – 1f – rhetoric

significat – 1 – s/he means, it means

studium, studiī – 2n – study

ubi – adv – where?

vult – irr – s/he wants

Grammatica Latīna

Making the Accusative case is easy. You take the Genetive case (2nd word) and lop off the Genitive ending. It works like this.

Accusative	Sing.
1st	-am
2nd M	-um
2nd N	-um
3rd M/F	-em
3rd N	_*
4th	-um
5th	-em

professōris ☞ professōr__ ☞ professōrem (yes, the macron)

librī ☞ libr__ ☞ librum

generis ☞ gener__ ☞ generem

We do all of this to get the Direct Object (DO). The reason we want to know how to do this is because we want to be able to make sentences with transitive verbs.

These are the sentences with a subject—SN, verb—Vt and direct object—DO.

	SN	VT	DO

Magister petit librum.
The teacher seeks the book.

	SN	DO	VT

Fīlia patrem spectat.
The daughter looks at father.

They're pretty basic sorts of sentences. And finally we also learned how to ask questions. It's mega easy.

Question word goes first in the question.

ADV LV PRN
<u>*Ubi*</u> *est Rōma?*
Where is Rome?

SN LV PRN
<u>*Quis*</u> *est magistra?*
Who is the teacher?

Pēnsa

Vōcēs memorandae
Fill in each blank with the definition supplied in *vōcēs*.

aperit – 4 – _____

casus, casūs – 4m – _____

cūr – adv – _____

dat – 1 – _____

exemplum, exemplī – 2n – _____

_____

facit –3io – _____

forma, formae – 1f – _____

genus, generis – 3f – _____

grammatica, grammaticae – 1f – _____

_____

habet – 2 – _____

invenit – 4 – _____

mittit – 3 – _____

nōmen, nōminis – 3n – _____

nōnne – adv – _____

_____

numerus, numerī – 2m – _____

_____

ostendit – 3 – _____

pōnit – 3 – _____

professor, professōris – 3m – _____

_____

quālis – adj (special) – _____

quandō – adv – _____

quid – pronoun – _____

quis – pronoun – _____

quō – adv – _____

quōmodo – adv – _____

quot – adv – _____

rhētorica, rhētoricae – 1f – _____

_____

significat – 1 – _____

studium, studiī – 2n – _____

ubi – adv – _____

vult – irr – _____

Derivative practice

Look for the Latin word in the *vōcēs* that goes with the English derivative. Then look the derivative up in your dictionary.

Latin word	English derivative	What the derivative means
	inventory	
	transmit	
	quality	
	studious	

What makes these go together?

Each group of Latin words has another Latin word in common. What is that word?

_____ 1. Quandō, Quid, Quō

_____ 2. Rhētorica, Grammatica, Studium

_____ 3. Ūnus, Duo, Trēs

_____ 4. Mittit, Dat

_____ 5. Docet, Liber, Studium

_____ 6. Casus, Numerus, Genus

a. Schola

b. Numerus

c. Professor

d. Dōnum

e. Nōmen

f. Rogat

Reading very short sentences

Read each sentence in Latin and label it.

1. Professor est pulcher.

2. Rēx ōrat.

3. Surgit homo.

Chapter 29
Going plural

Vōcēs

altus, alta, altum – adj – high
bonus, bona, bonum – adj – good
callidus, callida, callidum – adj – clever
clausus, clausa, clausum – adj – closed
doctus, docta, doctum – adj – educated
et – c – and
geminus, gemina, geminum – adj – twin
multus, multa, multum – adj – many
sunt – LV – they are
validus, valida, validum – adj – strong

Grammatica Latīna

Declension	Nominative Plural
1st	-ae
2nd M	-ī
2nd N	-a
3rd M/F	-ēs
3rd N	-a
4th	-ūs
5th	-ēs

This chapter is going to be a lot like chapter 22 crossed with chapter 25. First the bit like chapter 25. Instead of shifting to the Accusative case, we're going from singular to Nominative case plural. It works the same way—remember we start from the Genitive case!

fīliae ☞ fīli__ ☞ fīliae

manūs ☞ man__ ☞ manūs

librī ☞ libr__ ☞ librī

professōris ☞ professōr__ ☞ professōrēs

So it's super easy. (And really, all the other case/number combinations should be equally easy.)

Now for the chapter 22 bit. We're only going to work with the super irregular plural form of *est*. *Sunt*. It works the same, but it needs Nominative Plural nouns and adjectives.

SN　　LV　　PRA
Puerī sunt callidī.
The boys are clever.

ADJ　　LV　　PRN
Doctae sunt puellae.
The girls are educated.

Pēnsa

Vōcēs memorandae
Fill in each blank with the definition supplied in *vōcēs*.

altus, alta, altum – adj – _____

bonus, bona, bonum – adj – _____

callidus, callida, callidum – adj – _____

clausus, clausa, clausum – adj – _____

doctus, docta, doctum – adj – _____

et – c – _____

geminus, gemina, geminum – adj – _____

multus, multa, multum – adj – _____

sunt – LV – _____

validus, valida, validum – adj _____

Using the vōcēs
Circle the right answer.

1. Which one describes a weight lifter? Bonus Validus

2. Which one could describe a *porta*? Alta Clausa

3. Which one describes a *magistra*? Docta Et

4. Which one describes Romulus and Remus? Geminī Bonī

5. Which one can describe ants? Altus Multus

6. Which one better describes a basketball player? Altus Multus

7. Which one describes someone good at riddles? Callidus Sunt

8. If we've got a plural SN, which LV do we use? Est Sunt

Reading very short sentences

Say whether the LV is singular or plural in the blank. Then circle the right form of the PrA.

Singular ex. Frāter est ⬭altus⬭ altī

_____ 1. Matrēs sunt   bona   bonae

_____ 2. Magistrī sunt   doctus   doctī

_____ 3. Porta est   clausa   clausae

_____ 4. Oppidum est magnum magna

_____ 5. Puellae sunt   multa   multae

Derivative practice

Look for the Latin word in the _vōcēs_ that goes with the English derivative. Then look the derivative up in your dictionary.

Latin word	English derivative	What the derivative means
	altitude	
	clause	
	doctor	
	valid	

Probātiō

Vōcēs memoratae

Fill in the definition for each word.

altus, alta, altum – adj – _____

bonus, bona, bonum – adj – _____

callidus, callida, callidum – adj – _____

clausus, clausa, clausum – adj – _____

doctus, docta, doctum – adj – _____

et – c – _____

geminus, gemina, geminum – adj – _____

multus, multa, multum – adj – _____

sunt – LV – _____

validus, valida, validum – adj _____

Label the following sentences.

1. Callidī sunt discipulī.

2. Vir est validus.

Chapter 30
Word order

Vōcēs

anas, anatis – 3f – duck
avis, avis – 3If – bird
canis, canis – 3I m or f – dog
corvus, corvī – 2m – raven
fēlēs, fēlis – 3I m or f – cat
leō, leōnis – 3m – lion
mūs, muris – 3Im – mouse
taurus, taurī – 2m – bull
vaca, vacae – 1f – cow
vulpēs, vulpis – 3If – fox

Grammatica Latīna

The short answer to the question of word order in Latin is that it almost doesn't matter, and for what's in this book it doesn't. The longer answer is that word order is giving you information about what the speaker thinks is important in what they are saying—but that's advanced stuff.

Instead, I want to tell you what's normal. Latin sentences want to go in the order of SN-DO-Vt. It's kind of tricky for us English speakers, because we want SN-Vt-DO. The up side is that all of the case marking will help you get used to it.

   SN   DO   VT
Rēgīna vōcem habet.
The queen has a voice.

And by comparison, the same sentence in a not normal order.

   SN   VT   DO
Rēgīna habet vōcem.
The queen has a voice.

   VT   SN   DO
Habet rēgīna vōcem.
The queen has a voice.

These orders are both allowed and mean the same thing, but it is not exactly normal. Especially the order on the right. See how your attention is drawn to everything out of order? That's what word order changes do in Latin.

Pēnsa

Vōcēs memorandae
Fill in each blank with the definition supplied in *vōcēs*.

anas, anatis – 3f – _____

avis, avis – 3If – _____

canis, canis – 3I m or f – _____

corvus, corvī – 2m – _____

fēlēs, fēlis – 3I m or f – _____

leō, leōnis – 3m – _____

mūs, muris – 3Im – _____

taurus, taurī – 2m – _____

vaca, vacae – 1f – _____

vulpēs, vulpis – 3If – _____

Using the vōcēs
Circle the right answer.

1. Which one is an *avis*? Canis Corvus

2. Which one is a pet? Canis Vaca

3. Which one lives near water? Anas Mūs

4. Which one is in a bull fight? Leō Taurus

5. Which one purrs? Fēlēs Mūs

6. Which one is more like a fēlēs? Leō Taurus

7. Which one barks? Avis Canis

8. What's the usual order in sentences with Vt?

SN, Vt, DO	SN, DO, Vt	Vt, SN, DO	DO, Vt, SN

9. Draw a picture and label it with all of the *vōcēs*.

Derivative practice

Look for the Latin word in the *vōcēs* that goes with the English derivative. Then look the derivative up in your dictionary.

Latin word	English derivative	What the derivative means
	avian	
	feline	
	muscle	
	vaccine	

Probātiō

Vōcēs memorātae
Fill in the definition for each word.

anas, anatis – 3f – _____

avis, avis – 3If – _____

canis, canis – 3I m or f – _____

corvus, corvī – 2m – _____

fēlēs, fēlis – 3I m or f – _____

leō, leōnis – 3m – _____

mūs, muris – 3Im – _____

taurus, taurī – 2m – _____

vaca, vacae – 1f – _____

vulpēs, vulpis – 3If – _____

1. Write the labels for a transitive sentence in their usual order.

_____

Chapter 31
Two pronouns

Vōcēs

eam – pronoun – her/it (DO)
eum – pronoun – him/it (DO)
gladius, gladiī – 2m – sword
ignis, ignis – 3If – fire
inopia, inopiae – 1f – lack
modus, modī – 2m – way
mors, mortis – 3f – death
nāvis, nāvis – 3If – ship
valē – idiom – good bye!
vocat – 1 – s/he calls

Grammatica Latīna

Like English, Latin has pronouns. I've been avoiding them up to now. Why? They're hard to draw. And they don't have obvious derivatives in English. The problem is that they're really common. How common? Well, think about how long you could go without saying he, him, she, her, it, they or them. Give it a try. You won't last long, because they're common. Here is how they work.

1. Identify the noun you want to replace.

2. Note its case, number and gender.
     This step is important. For now, case, number and gender should match.

3. Find the pronoun that matches in case, number and gender.

4. Replace the noun.

Here's an example.

SN	DO	VT

Magistra ignem videt.
The teacher sees the fire.

SN	DO	VT

Magistra eum videt.
The teacher sees it.

As you can see, gender has a somewhat strange effect.

Pēnsa

Vōcēs memorandae
Fill in each blank with the definition supplied in *vōcēs*.

eam – pronoun – _____

eum – pronoun – _____

gladius, gladiī – 2m – _____

ignis, ignis – 3If – _____

inopia, inopiae – 1f – _____

modus, modī – 2m – _____

mors, mortis – 3f – _____

nāvis, nāvis – 3If – _____

valē – idiom – _____

vocat – 1 – _____

Using the vōcēs
Circle the right answer.

1. 1. Which one would you rather have in the ocean? Gladius Nāvis

2. If you have *nihil*, what else might you have? Ignis Inopia

3. If you shout someone's *nōmen*, what are you doing? Mors Vocat

4. How might you refer to me without using my name? Eum Mors

5. If you have a way you like doing things, what do you have? Ignis Modus

6. How might you refer to your mother without using her name? Eam Eum

7. Hey, we're almost done with the book. What should we say? Valē Vocat

8. Do pronouns match their nouns in case, number and gender? Yes No

Reading very short sentences
Read the sentence in Latin and match it with the sentence without the pronoun.

_____1. Ignis eum vocat.

_____2. Gladius eum videt.

_____3. Gladius eum nōn videt.

_____4. Gladius tacet.

_____5. Ignis eum nōn videt.

a.Gladius ignem nōn videt.

b. No pronoun in sentence.

c. Ignis gladium vocat.

d. Ignis gladium nōn videt.

e. Gladius ignem videt.

Derivative practice

Look for the Latin word in the *vōcēs* that goes with the English derivative. Then look the derivative up in your dictionary.

Latin word	English derivative	What the derivative means
	gladiator	
	ignition	
	mortal	
	vocal	

Probātiō

Vōcēs memorātae

Fill in the definition for each word.

eam – pronoun – _____

eum – pronoun – _____

gladius, gladiī – 2m – _____

ignis, ignis – 3If – _____

inopia, inopiae – 1f – _____

modus, modī – 2m – _____

mors, mortis – 3f – _____

nāvis, nāvis – 3If – _____

valē – idiom – _____

vocat – 1 – _____

Label the following stentences.

1. Cūr ignis eum vocat?

2. Ignis eum amat.

Vōcēs

altus, alta, altum – adj – high

anas, anatis – 3f – duck

avis, avis – 3If – bird

bonus, bona, bonum – adj
  – good

callidus, callida, callidum – adj
  – clever

canis, canis – 3I m or f – dog

clausus, clausa, clausum – adj
  – closed

corvus, corvī – 2m – raven

doctus, docta, doctum – adj
  – educated

eam – pronoun – her/it (DO)

et – c – and

eum – pronoun – him/it (DO)

fēlēs, fēlis – 3I m or f – cat

geminus, gemina, geminum
  – adj – twin

gladius, gladiī – 2m – sword

ignis, ignis – 3If – fire

inopia, inopiae – 1f – lack

leō, leōnis – 3m – lion

modus, modī – 2m – way

mors, mortis – 3f – death

multus, multa, multum – adj
  – many

mūs, muris – 3Im – mouse

nāvis, nāvis – 3If – ship

sunt – LV – they are

taurus, taurī – 2m – bull

vaca, vacae – 1f – cow

valē – idiom – good bye!

validus, valida, validum – adj
  – strong

vocat – 1 – s/he calls

vulpēs, vulpis – 3If – fox

Grammatica Latīna

This time we didn't change case, we changed number. Bring on the Nominative plural! It works the same way as moving to the Accusative case. Find the Genitive, take off the ending and add on the new ending. Voila!

Nominative	Plural
1st	-ae
2nd M	-ī
2nd N	-a
3rd M/F	-ēs
3rd N	-a
4th	-ūs
5th	-ēs

fīliae ☞ fīli__ ☞ fīliae

manūs ☞ man__ ☞ manūs

librī ☞ libr__ ☞ librī

professōris ☞ professōr__ ☞ professōrēs

Of course plural nouns mean we can't use *est* any more. Bring on *sunt*. It's just like *est*, but needs Nominative Plural nouns and adjectives, which we have conveniently learned.

SN   LV   PRA
Puerī sunt callidī.
The boys are clever.

ADJ   SN   PRN
Doctae sunt puellae.
The girls are educated.

We also learned the usual word order for transitive sentences. This order is good to know because Latin can be really tricky with word order.

SN   DO   VT
Rēgīna vōcem habet.
The queen has a voice.

And we also learned about two pronouns in Latin. Here's how to figure out which one you will want.

1. *Identify the noun you want to replace.*

2. *Note its case, number and gender (this step is important).*

3. *Find the pronoun that matches in case, number and gender.*

4. *Replace the noun.*

Here's how it works.

SN   DO   VT
Magistra <u>ignem</u> videt.
The teacher sees the fire.

SN   DO   VT
Magistra <u>eum</u> videt.
The teacher sees it.

Pēnsa

Vōcēs memorandae

Fill in each blank with the definition supplied in *vōcēs*.

altus, alta, altum – adj – _____

anas, anatis – 3f – _____

avis, avis – 3If – _____

bonus, bona, bonum – adj – _____

_____

callidus, callida, callidum – adj – _____

_____

canis, canis – 3m&f – _____

clausus, clausa, clausum – adj – _____

_____

corvus, corvī – 2m – _____

doctus, docta, doctum – adj – _____

_____

eam – pronoun – _____

et – c – _____

eum – pronoun – _____

fēlēs, fēlis – 3m&f – _____

geminus, gemina, geminum – adj – ___

_____

gladius, gladiī – 2m – _____

ignis, ignis – 3If – _____

inopia, inopiae – 1f – _____

leō, leōnis – 3m – _____

modus, modī – 2m – _____

mors, mortis – 3f – _____

multus, multa, multum – adj – _____

_____

mūs, muris – 3m – _____

nāvis, nāvis – 3If – _____

sunt – LV – _____

taurus, taurī – 2m – _____

vaca, vacae – 1f – _____

valē – idiom – _____

validus, valida, validum – adj – _____

_____

vocat – 1 – _____

Derivative practice

Look for the Latin word in the *vōcēs* that goes with the English derivative. Then look the derivative up in your dictionary.

Latin word	English derivative	What the derivative means
	ignite	
	mortuary	
	prepared	
	altimiter	

What makes these go together?

Each word on the left goes with a word on the right. What is that word?

_____ 1. Amor   a. Amat

_____ 2. Doctus   b. Vīvit

_____ 3. Dux   c. Vocat

_____ 4. Vīta   d. Docet

_____ 5. Vox   e. Dūcit

Reading very short sentences

Read each sentence in Latin and label it.

1. Geminī sunt frātrēs.

2. Rōma vocat eum.

3. Gladius nōn est acūtus.

Chapter by chapter
Word list

Chapter 1 *Vōcēs*

familia, familiae – 1f – family
fēmina, fēminae – 1f – woman
frāter, frātris – 3m – brother
māter, mātris – 3f – mother
parēns, parentis – 3m/f – parent
pater, patris – 3m – father
puella, puellae – 1f – girl
puer, puerī – 2m – boy
soror, sorōris – 3f – sister
vir, virī – 2m – man

Chapter 2 *Vōcēs*

discipula, discipulae – 1f – student (girl)
discipulus, discipulī – 2m – student (boy)
fābula, fābulae – 1f – story
historia, historiae – 1f – history
liber, librī – 2m – book
magister, magistrī – 2m – teacher (man)
magistra, magistrae – 1f – teacher (woman)
penna, pennae – 1f – pen
schola, scholae – 1f – school
sella, sellae – 1f – chair

Chapter 3 *Vōcēs*

ager, agrī – 2m – field
aqua, aquae – 1f – water
arbor, arboris – 3f – tree
flōs, flōris – 3m – flower
fluvius, fluviī – 2m – river
īnsula, īnsulae – 1f – island
oceanus, oceanī – 2m – ocean
sōl, sōlis – 3m – sun
urbs, urbis – 3If – city
via, viae – 1f – road

Chapter 5 *Vōcēs*

aestās, aestātis – 3f – summer
annus, annī – 2m – year
diēs, diēī – 5m – day
hodiē – adv – today
māne – 3n – morning
meridiēs, meridiēī – 5m – noon
nox, noctis – 3f – night
prīmus, prīma, prīmum – adj – first
tempus, temporis – 3n – time
ultimus, ultima, ultimum – adj – last

Chapter 6 *Vōcēs*

auctor, auctōris – 3m – author
captīvus, captīvī – 2m – prisoner
dux, ducis – 3m – leader
mīles, mīlitis – 3m – soldier
nauta, nautae – 1m – sailor
poeta, poetae – 1m –poet
rēgīna, rēgīnae – 1f – queen
rēx, rēgis – 3m – king
scriptor, scriptōris – 3m – writer
uxor, uxōris – 3f – wife

Chapter 7 *Vōcēs*

casa, casae – 1f –house
cēna, cēnae – 1f – supper
cibus, cibī – 2m – food
cista, cistae – 1f – box
cubiculum, cubiculī – 2n – bedroom
culīna, culīnae – 1f – kitchen
fructus, fructūs – 4m – fruit
lectus, lectī – 2m – bed
mēnsa, mēnsae – 1f – table
porta, portae – 1f – gate

Chapter 9 Vōcēs

caelum, caelī – 2n – sky
ecclēsia, ecclēsiae – 1f – church
equus, equī – 2m – horse
fōns, fontis – 3m – fountain
fundus, fundī – 2m – farm
negōtium, negōtiī – 2n – business
oppidum, oppidī – 2n – town
portus, portūs – 4m – port
rūs, rūris – 3n – country
templum, templī – 2n – temple

Chapter 10 Vōcēs

ars, artis – 3f – skill
auxilium, auxiliī – 2n – help
causa, causae – 1f – cause
cōnsilium, cōnsiliī – 2n – plan
dōnum, dōnī – 2n – gift
epistula, epistulae – 1f – letter
nihil – n – nothing
perīculum, perīculī – 2n – danger
respōnsum, respōnsī – 2n – answer
verbum, verbī – 2n – word

Chapter 11 Vōcēs

corpus, corporis – 3n – body
digitus, digitī – 2m – finger
faciēs, faciēī –5f – face
lingua, linguae – 1f – tongue
manus, manūs – 4f – hand
memoria, memoriae – 1f – memory
oculus, oculī – 2m – eye
pēs, pedis – 3m – foot
vox, vōcis – 3f – voice
vultus, vultūs – 4m – face

Chapter 13 Vōcēs

ūnus, ūna, ūnum – adj irregular – one
duo, duae, duo – adj irregular – two
trēs, trēs, tria – adj irregular – three
quattuor – adj indeclinable – four
quīnque – adj indeclinable – five
sex – adj indeclinable – six
septem – adj indeclinable – seven
octo – adj indeclinable – eight
novem – adj indeclinable – nine
decem – adj indeclinable – ten

Chapter 14 Vōcēs

agit – 3 – s/he does
audit – 4 – s/he hears
dīcit – 3 – s/he says
docet – 2 – s/he teaches
est – LV – s/he is
inquit – irr – s/he says
legit –3 – s/he reads
ōrat – 1 – s/he prays
rogat – 1 – s/he asks
tacet – 2 – s/he is quiet

Chapter 15 Vōcēs

cadit – 3 – s/he falls
currit – 3 – s/he runs
dūcit – 3 – s/he leads
fert – irr – s/he carries
it – irr – s/he goes
parat – 1 – s/he prepares
petit – 3 – s/he seeks
sedet – 2 – s/he sits
surgit – 3 – s/he gets up
venit – 4 – s/he comes

Chapter 17 Vōcēs

acus, acūs – 4m – needle
carmen, carminis – 2n – song
cūra, cūrae – 1f – care
ludus, ludī – 2m – game
mundus, mundī – 2m – world
nātūra, ae – 1f –nature
nōmen, nōminis – 3n – name
pars, partis – 3f – part
quaestiō, quaestiōnis – 3f – question
rēs, reī –5f – thing

Chapter 18 Vōcēs

cīvitās, cīvitātis – 3f – citizenship
cōnsul, cōnsulis – 3m – consul (Roman political leader)
gēns, gentis – 3f – tribe
imperium, imperiī – 2n – empire
latīnus, latīna, latīnum – adj – Latin
nātus, nātūs – 4m – birth
populus, populī – 2m – people
Rōma, Rōmae – 1f – Rome
Rōmānus, Rōmāna, Rōmānum – adj – Roman
Senātus, Senātūs – 4m – Senate

Chapter 19 Vōcēs

amor, amōris – 3m – love
animus, animī – 2m – soul, mind
deus, deī – 2m – god
dominus, dominī – 2m – lord
fidēs, fideī – 5f – faith
glōria, glōriae – 1f – glory
munus, muneris – 3n – job, gift
pecūnia, pecūniae – 1f – money
rēgnum, rēgnī – 2n – kingdom
spīritus, spīritūs – 4m – spirit

Chapter 21 Vōcēs

amīca, amīcae – 1f – friend (girl, woman)
amīcus, amīcī – 2m –friend (boy, man)
fīlia, fīliae – 1f – daughter
fīlius, fīliī – 2m – son
homo, hominis – 3m – human
nōn – adv – not
nuntius, nuntiī – 2m – messenger
rosa, rosae – 1f – rose
spina, spinae – 1f – thorn
vīta, vītae – 1f – life

Chapter 22 Vōcēs

aeger, aegra, aegrum – adj – sick
astūtus, astūta, astūtum – adj – clever
carus, cara, carum – adj – dear
lentus, lenta, lentum – adj – slow
magnus, magna, magnum – adj – big, great
meus, mea, meum – adj – my, mine
noster, nostra, nostrum – adj – our
pulcher, pulchra, pulchrum – adj – beautiful
tuus, tua, tuum – adj – your, yours
vester, vestra, vestrum – adj – yours (pl)

Chapter 23 Vōcēs

amat – 1 – s/he loves
cognōscit – 3 – s/he knows
horrēscit – 3 – s/he gets scared
-ne – ? – asks yes/no question
nescit – 4 – s/he does not know
putat – 1 – s/he thinks
spectat – 1 – s/he looks at
timet – 2 – s/he fears
videt – 2 – s/he sees
vīvit – 4 – s/he lives

Chapter 25 Vōcēs

casus, casūs – 4m – case
exemplum, exemplī – 2n – example
forma, formae – 1f – shape
genus, generis – 3f – gender
grammatica, grammaticae – 1f – grammar
nōmen, nōminis – 3n – noun
numerus, numerī – 2m – number
professor, professōris – 3m – professor
rhētorica, rhētoricae – 1f – rhetoric
studium, studiī – 2n – study

Chapter 26 Vōcēs

aperit – 4 – s/he opens
dat – 1 – s/he gives
facit –3io – s/he makes
habet – 2 – s/he has
invenit – 4 – s/he finds
mittit – 3 – s/he sends
ostendit – 3 – s/he holds out
pōnit – 3 – s/he places
significat – 1 – s/he means
vult – irr – s/he wants

Chapter 27 Vōcēs

cūr – adv – why?
nōnne – adv – asks question expecting yes
    answer
quālis – adj (special) – what kind?
quandō – adv – when?
quid – pronoun – what?
quis – pronoun – who?
quō – adv – where to?
quōmodo – adv – how?
quot – adv – how many?
ubi – adv – where?

Chapter 29 Vōcēs

altus, alta, altum – adj – high
bonus, bona, bonum – adj – good
callidus, callida, callidum – adj – clever
clausus, clausa, clausum – adj – closed
doctus, docta, doctum – adj – educated
et – c – and
geminus, gemina, geminum – adj – twin
multus, multa, multum – adj – many
sunt – LV – they are
validus, valida, validum – adj – strong

Chapter 30 Vōcēs

anas, anatis – 3f – duck
avis, avis – 3If – bird
canis, canis – 3I m or f – dog
corvus, corvī – 2m – raven
fēlēs, fēlis – 3I m or f – cat
leō, leōnis – 3m – lion
mūs, muris – 3Im – mouse
taurus, taurī – 2m – bull
vaca, vacae – 1f – cow
vulpēs, vulpis – 3If – fox

Chapter 31 Vōcēs

eam – pronoun – her/it (DO)
eum – pronoun – him/it (DO)
gladius, gladiī – 2m – sword
ignis, ignis – 3If – fire
inopia, inopiae – 1f – lack
modus, modī – 2m – way
mors, mortis – 3f – death
nāvis, nāvis – 3If – ship
valē – idiom – good bye!
vocat – 1 – s/he calls

Glossary

These are all of the words that appear in this book in alphabetical order.

A

acus, acūs – 4m – needle

aeger, aegra, aegrum – adj – sick

aestās, aestātis – 3f – summer

ager, agrī – 2m – field

agit – 3 – s/he does

altus, alta, altum – adj – high

amat – 1 – s/he loves

amīca, amīcae – 1f – friend (girl, woman)

amīcus, amīcī – 2m –friend (boy, man)

amor, amōris – 3m – love

animus, animī – 2m – soul, mind

anas, anatis – 3f – duck

annus, annī – 2m – year

aperit – 4 – s/he opens

aqua, aquae – 1f – water

arbor, arboris – 3f – tree

ars, artis – 3f – skill

astūtus, astūta, astūtum – adj – clever

auctor, auctōris – 3m – author

audit – 4 – s/he hears

auxilium, auxiliī – 2n – help

avis, avis – 3If – bird

B

bonus, bona, bonum – adj – good

C

cadit – 3 – s/he falls

caelum, caelī – 2n – sky

callidus, callida, callidum – adj – clever

canis, canis – 3I m or f – dog

captīvus, captīvī – 2m – prisoner

carmen, carminis – 2n – song

carus, cara, carum – adj – dear

casa, casae – 1f –house

casus, casūs – 4m – case

causa, causae – 1f – cause

cēna, cēnae – 1f – supper

cibus, cibī – 2m – food

cista, cistae – 1f – box

cīvitās, cīvitātis – 3f – citizenship

clausus, clausa, clausum – adj – closed

cognōscit – 3 – s/he knows

cōnsilium, cōnsiliī – 2n – plan

cōnsul, cōnsulis – 3m – consul (Roman political leader)

corpus, corporis – 3n – body

corvus, corvī – 2m – raven

cubiculum, cubiculī – 2n – bedroom

culīna, culīnae – 1f – kitchen

cūr – adv – why?

cūra, cūrae – 1f – care

currit – 3 – s/he runs

D

dat – 1 – s/he gives

decem – adj indeclinable – ten

deus, deī – 2m – god

dīcit – 3 – s/he says

diēs, diēī – 5m – day

digitus, digitī – 2m – finger

discipula, discipulae – 1f – student (girl)

discipulus, discipulī – 2m – student (boy)

docet – 2 – s/he teaches

doctus, docta, doctum – adj – educated

dominus, dominī – 2m – lord

dōnum, dōnī – 2n – gift

dūcit – 3 – s/he leads

duo, duae, duo – adj irregular – two

dux, ducis – 3m – leader

E

eam – pronoun – her/it (DO)

ecclēsia, ecclēsiae – 1f – church

epistula, epistulae – 1f – letter

equus, equī – 2m – horse

est – LV – s/he is

et – c – and

eum – pronoun – him/it (DO)

exemplum, exemplī – 2n – example

F

fābula, fābulae – 1f – story
faciēs, faciēī –5f – face
facit –3io – s/he makes
familia, familiae – 1f – family
fēlēs, fēlis – 3I m or f – cat
fēmina, fēminae – 1f – woman
fert – irr – s/he carries
fidēs, fideī – 5f – faith
fīlia, fīliae – 1f – daughter
fīlius, fīliī – 2m – son
flōs, flōris – 3m – flower
fluvius, fluviī – 2m – river
fōns, fontis – 3m – fountain
forma, formae – 1f – shape
frāter, frātris – 3m – brother
fructus, fructūs – 4m – fruit
fundus, fundī – 2m – farm

G

geminus, gemina, geminum – adj – twin
gēns, gentis – 3f – tribe
genus, generis – 3f – gender
gladius, gladiī – 2m – sword
glōria, glōriae – 1f – glory
grammatica, grammaticae – 1f – grammar

H

habet – 2 – s/he has
historia, historiae – 1f – history
hodiē – adv – today
homo, hominis – 3m – human
horrēscit – 3 – s/he gets scared

I

ignis, ignis – 3If – fire
imperium, imperiī – 2n – empire
inopia, inopiae – 1f – lack
inquit – irr – s/he says
īnsula, īnsulae – 1f – island
invenit – 4 – s/he finds
it – irr – s/he goes

L

latīnus, latīna, latīnum – adj – Latin

lectus, lectī – 2m – bed
legit –3 – s/he reads
lentus, lenta, lentum – adj – slow
leō, leōnis – 3m – lion
liber, librī – 2m – book
lingua, linguae – 1f – tongue
ludus, ludī – 2m – game

M

magister, magistrī – 2m – teacher (man)
magistra, magistrae – 1f – teacher (woman)
magnus, magna, magnum – adj – big, great
māne – 3n – morning
manus, manūs – 4f – hand
māter, mātris – 3f – mother
memoria, memoriae – 1f – memory
mēnsa, mēnsae – 1f – table
meridiēs, meridiēī – 5m – noon
meus, mea, meum – adj – my, mine
mīles, mīlitis – 3m – soldier
mittit – 3 – s/he sends
modus, modī – 2m – way
mors, mortis – 3f – death
multus, multa, multum – adj – many
mundus, mundī – 2m – world
munus, muneris – 3n – job, gift
mūs, muris – 3Im – mouse

N

nātūra, ae – 1f –nature
nātus, nātūs – 4m – birth
nauta, nautae – 1m – sailor
nāvis, nāvis – 3If – ship
-ne – ? – asks yes/no question
negōtium, negōtiī – 2n – business
nescit – 4 – s/he does not know
nihil – n – nothing
nōmen, nōminis – 3n – name
nōmen, nōminis – 3n – noun
nōn – adv – not
nōnne – adv – asks question expecting yes
   answer
noster, nostra, nostrum – adj – noun
novem – adj indeclinable – nine
nox, noctis – 3f – night

numerus, numerī – 2m – number
nuntius, nuntiī – 2m – messenger

O

oceanus, oceanī – 2m – ocean
octo – adj indeclinable – eight
oculus, oculī – 2m – eye
oppidum, oppidī – 2n – town
ōrat – 1 – s/he prays
ostendit – 3 – s/he holds out

P

parat – 1 – s/he prepares
parēns, parentis – 3m/f – parent
pars, partis – 3f – part
pater, patris – 3m – father
pecūnia, pecūniae – 1f – money
penna, pennae – 1f – pen
perīculum, perīculī – 2n – danger
pēs, pedis – 3m – foot
petit – 3 – s/he seeks
poeta, poetae – 1m –poet
pōnit – 3 – s/he places
populus, populī – 2m – people
porta, portae – 1f – gate
portus, portūs – 4m – port
prīmus, prīma, prīmum – adj – first
professor, professōris – 3m – professor
puella, puellae – 1f – girl
puer, puerī – 2m – boy
pulcher, pulchra, pulchrum – adj –
    beautiful
putat – 1 – s/he thinks

Q

quaestiō, quaestiōnis – 3f – question
quālis – adj (special) – what kind?
quandō – adv – when?
quattuor – adj indeclinable – four
quid – pronoun – what?
quīnque – adj indeclinable – five
quis – pronoun – who?
quō – adv – where to?
quōmodo – adv – how?
quot – adv – how many?

R

rēgina, rēginae – 1f – queen
rēgnum, rēgnī – 2n – kingdom
rēs, reī –5f – thing
respōnsum, respōnsī – 2n – answer
rēx, rēgis – 3m – king
rhētorica, rhētoricae – 1f – rhetoric
rogat – 1 – s/he asks
Rōma, Rōmae – 1f – Rome
Rōmānus, Rōmāna, Rōmānum – adj –
    Roman
rosa, rosae – 1f – rose
rūs, rūris – 3n – country

S

schola, scholae – 1f – school
scriptor, scriptōris – 3m – writer
sedet – 2 – s/he sits
sella, sellae – 1f – chair
Senātus, Senātūs – 4m – Senate
septem – adj indeclinable – seven
sex – adj indeclinable – six
significat – 1 – s/he means
sōl, sōlis – 3m – sun
soror, sorōris – 3f – sister
spectat – 1 – s/he looks at
spina, spinae – 1f – thorn
spīritus, spīritūs – 4m – spirit
studium, studiī – 2n – study
sunt – LV – they are
surgit – 3 – s/he gets up

T

tacet – 2 – s/he is quiet
taurus, taurī – 2m – bull
templum, templī – 2n – temple
tempus, temporis – 3n – time
timet – 2 – s/he fears
trēs, trēs, tria – adj irregular – three
tuus, tua, tuum – adj – your, yours

U

ubi – adv – where?
ultimus, ultima, ultimum – adj – last

ūnus, ūna, ūnum – adj irregular – one
urbs, urbis – 3If – city
uxor, uxōris – 3f – wife

V

vaca, vacae – 1f – cow
valē – idiom – good bye!
validus, valida, validum – adj – strong
venit – 4 – s/he comes
verbum, verbī – 2n – word
vester, vestra, vestrum – adj – yours (pl)
via, viae – 1f – road

videt – 2 – s/he sees
vir, virī – 2m – man
vīta, vītae – 1f – life
vīvit – 4 – s/he lives
vocat – 1 – s/he calls
vox, vōcis – 3f – voice
vulpēs, vulpis – 3If – fox
vult – irr – s/he wants
vultus, vultūs – 4m – face

Made in the USA
Las Vegas, NV
23 February 2022